great escapes

D0283025

LONG ISLAND

great ESCAPES

Weekend Getaways

Nature Hideaways

Day Trips

Easy Planning

Best Places to Visit

Steven Howell

LONG ISLAND

The Countryman Press • Woodstock, Vermont

DEDICATION

This book is dedicated to Officer Kenneth Baribault and his loyal and loving family: Ken, Jennifer, Danielle, and my dear cousin Patricia. You are the epitome of Long Island uncompromised strength, generous spirit, and unequivocal love in the face of adversity. God bless you all on your long road to recovery.

We welcome your comments and suggestions. Please contact Editor, The Countryman Press, P.O. Box 748, Woodstock, Vermont 05091, or e-mail countrymanpress@wwnorton.com.

ISBN 978-0-88150-875-8

Cover photos by Steven Howell
Interior photographs by the author unless otherwise specified
Map by Paul Woodward, © The Countryman Press
Book design by Bodenweber Design
Text composition by Chelsea Cloeter

Published by The Countryman Press
P.O. Box 748
Woodstock, Vermont 05091

Distributed by W. W. Norton & Company, Inc.
500 Fifth Avenue
New York, NY 10110

Printed in the United States of America

10 9 8 7 6 5 4 3 2 1

ACKNOWLEDGMENTS

Very special thanks go to:

Jennifer Bedell-Darienzo—travel companion extraordinaire. Funchos to you!

My favorite family from Long Island: Neal, Bob, Jenny, Bobby, and Emily Citro—sincere thanks for the crash pad and always keeping me very well fed! You are a beautiful family.

To Lévi Bérubé—thanks for your understanding and patience come deadline time!

To family and friends—the Stewarts and the Determanns in particular—who suggested some great restaurant, sightseeing, and hotel recommendations.

My friends and colleagues at Countryman Press, including Kermit Hummel, Lisa Sacks, Kim Grant, and Susan Barnett for her copyediting prowess.

Public relations professionals throughout Long Island.

To all the fine Long Islanders I interviewed for this book—thank you for your valuable time and insight. I could not have done this without you.

And to Johnny, Brenda, and Marie—it's always great to see you. And to Jillian-Marie—it's always fun to watch Charlie Brown at Halloween and play Barbie cruise ship/*Poseidon Adventure* with you. —Love, Uncle Steven

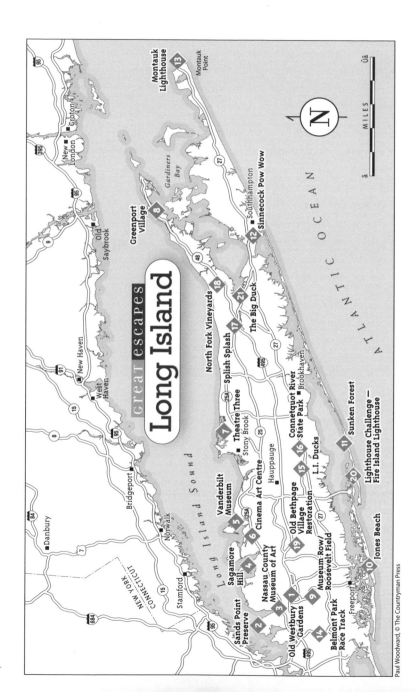

great escapes

Long Island

Sands Point Preserve

Saganore Hill

Vanderbilt Museum

Greenport Village

Montauk Lighthouse

North Fork Vineyards

Splish Splash

The Big Duck

Sinnecock Pow Wow

Southampton

Theatre Three

Stony Brook

Nassau County Museum of Art

Cinema Art Centre

Hauppauge

Old Bethpage Village Restoration

Connetquot River State Park

Brookhaven

L.I. Ducks

Sunken Forest

Museum Row/ Roosevelt Field

Old Westbury Gardens

Jones Beach

Belmont Park Race Track

Freeport

Lighthouse Challenge— Fire Island Lighthouse

ATLANTIC OCEAN

Long Island Sound

Gardiners Bay

New London

Groton

Old Saybrook

New Haven

West Haven

Bridgeport

Norwalk

Stamford

Danbury

NEW YORK

CONNECTICUT

MILES

N

Paul Woodward, © The Countryman Press

CONTENTS

Unique—Long Island—New York

Long Island geographically speaking: Nassau and Suffolk Counties

Welcome to Long Island. Which one? Geographically speaking, Long Island measures about 115 miles long from Manhattan to Montauk Point. This, of course, includes the New York City boroughs of Queens and Brooklyn. But to a local, and for the purposes of this book, Long Island starts at the Queens/Nassau border. This book is all about Nassau and Suffolk counties.

I am one of those LIers who have moved away (I've been told I have a "Lawn Guyland" accent—"cawfee," that hot beverage you have with breakfast, is a big giveaway), but most of my family and friends still live here, so I visit often. For this book, it was quite a fun adventure to rediscover the best that Long Island has to offer and to also reinforce the idea that "suburbia" ain't such a bad word after all—I wear the suburbanite moniker proudly. Here's hoping you relive your own little slice of suburban heaven—Long Island—style. I know I have.

Now if it weren't for all that traffic...

How to use this book

This is not an all-inclusive tourist tome on Long Island but a loosely themed, lighthearted, and quirky look at some of its finer moments.

Need to get away but are short on time? Your staycation is most definitely in your own backyard. Here are some recommended Long Island visits geared for day-trippers, the workday weary, and those in search of a surprising weekend getaway close to home.

Think of each chapter as its own suggested itinerary. The chapters highlight a specific Long Island destination followed by a roundup of pertinent travel info such as how to get there, suggested restaurants, shopping, and sightseeing in the same vicinity as the main story, mostly a town or two away. Many of the highlighted stories in each chapter are open or accessible year-round. Some are seasonal; some are special events that last but a weekend every year, such as the Shinnecock Powwow and the Sands Point Medieval Fair. That said, you can still visit the accompanying roundup entries in those chapters any time of year.

Since you're on Long Island, most chapters feature a "waterfront" listing, anything from a tranquil pond to an invigorating ocean view, all specifically meant as a place to kick back, pack a picnic lunch (when was the last time you did that?), and calm your hurried commuter nerves. The water—from the Long Island Sound to the Atlantic Ocean—is, after all, one of the main reasons why locals live on and visitors visit Long Island.

The roundup will also include special events within a certain area, driving tips, local resources, a LIRR option for those out-of-towners (or even LIers who wish to ditch the car for a day), a fun fact or two, and where to explore nearby if you have more time. Please check the front map to create your own itinerary and combine activities in a specific geographic area.

A word of note about listed prices for restaurants, hotels, attractions, and taxicabs: the prices listed are approximate to winter 2010.

As for the restaurants, everyone's a critic, right? Me, not so much. I prefer to tell you what's where and why I liked it, but I won't tell you what you should like (that goes for the sightseeing visits as well). So restaurant listings are not outright reviews—I've eaten at many, but not all—but most of the restaurants were at least visited, researched, and/or recommended by family and friends. Exact establishment hours are not given, because they sometimes change. Call ahead for hours and always make a reservation.

Taxi service on Long Island differs from New York City–style cabs. The price given is not per cab ride but per person. There is often an extra charge for additional passengers.

Since my best friends, Neal and Bob, don't rent their home to strangers—and it's where I stay when in town—many hotels in this book are suggested in terms of geography. Some were visited as a walk-through, and others came recommended by family and friends. As for hotels, shop around for the best deal as online price quotes vary greatly from season to season. Money-saving tips to consider include the purchase of an Empire Passport, a Nassau County Leisure Pass, and a Suffolk County GreenKey, which all offer reduced admission to area parks. Check "Everything Else You Need to Know" in the appendix of this book for more information on each.

Although some of the chapter groupings of towns may seem a bit unconventional, they are simply suggestions to point you in a particular direction. A few chapters are devoted to their own drive/tour itineraries, such as the Long Island Lighthouse Challenge, a North Fork winery tour, and a Great South Bay estates tour. There's a method to my Long Island madness. And that method is akin to the rhythmic Atlantic Ocean tide: just go with the Long Island flow and, most of all, have a good time.

GOLD COAST
TREASURES

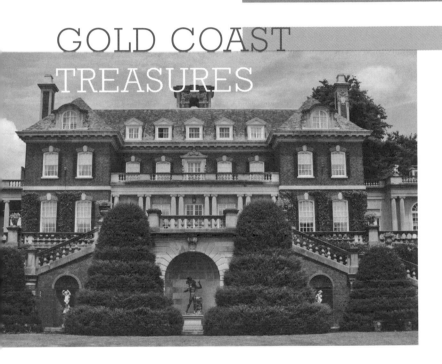

1 • LIGHTS, CAMERA, ACTION IN OLD WESTBURY: *Old Westbury Gardens*

Old Westbury, Albertson, Williston Park, North Hills, Carle Place, Jericho

A stately, ornate black wrought-iron gate offers the first clue of grandeur. Its intricate pattern, curving skyward this way and that, demonstrates the care taken by the meticulous and patient hands of a skilled craftsman. Except for their color, the gold initials JSP might get lost in the detail. Just past the entrance—the tight squeeze means SUVs should proceed with caution—two double rows of expertly trimmed European linden trees flank each side of a grand landscaped allée. The entry alone says you've arrived in elegant style, but the best is yet to come.

Situated on 200 acres, Old Westbury Gardens was the former home of John "Jay" S. Phipps. Of all of Long Island's great estates, this one didn't quite fit into the Gold Coast category, says Vincent Kish, the director of public relations and communications.

"This one's a little south of the traditional Glen Cove, Oyster Bay, or Little Neck estates," Kish said. "Phipps was a big horseman, and he preferred the area's flat terrain. So we call it a North Shore estate rather than a Gold Coast one."

Kish says that the Charles II–style Westbury House was constructed between 1904 and 1906. The Phipps family moved in the following year. But it wasn't the grand mansion that sealed a wedding deal.

The story goes that Phipps, whose family fortune came from banking and steel— his dad Henry was a partner of Andrew Carnegie of U.S. Steel fame—went to England to ask for the hand in marriage of Margarita Grace, an heir to the W. R. Grace shipping lines.

"Between the two, they weren't clipping coupons," Kish quips.

When the American Phipps was courting the British Grace in England, he promised to build her an English-style country house complete with garden reminiscent of her home in England.

"So we think the basic design of this garden is what Margarita had growing up in England," Kish said. "That was part of the deal of how he wooed her."

It worked. Phipps and Grace married and raised four children in Westbury, three boys and the youngest, Peggie, who lived on

Hildebrandt's

Old Westbury Gardens Arch

the property in a separate 1859 Quaker farmhouse in her later life. She only recently passed away in 2006 at the age of 99.

"She essentially never left the Long Island estate," Kish said. "She used to get around the grounds with a golf cart. She'd often walk the grounds, and visitors would have no clue as to who she was."

Kish recalls bringing his own family to the gardens for a visit. One time his young son decided to enjoy the simple adventure of climbing a tree.

"Peggie came by and said, 'Hey, get out of my tree!'"

Kish's wife had to explain to the youngster who Peggie was.

The centerpiece 2½-acre garden remains the heart of the Old Westbury estate. By the end of May the tranquil space is awash in a rainbow of primrose and azaleas. The hybrid roses peak in June but last well into October. Fall promises another spectacular show of color. As with many great Long Island estates, a fancy mansion and a garden of delights also attracts any number of movie and television productions, advertising photographers, and wedding processions, which all provide a generous source of income.

So where have you seen Old Westbury Gardens before?

Alfred Hitchcock's *North by Northwest* was the first of 18 movies to have been filmed here since the 1950s. Archival photos show Cary Grant enjoying the grounds.

Westbury House doubled as Ryan O'Neal's family home in *Love Story* and its sequel, *Oliver's Story*. Woody Allen paid a visit and used the property in *The Jade Scorpion*. Denzel Washington and Armand Assante recently went head-to-head at Old Westbury for the film *American Gangster*.

"And Susan Sarandon died in that bed," Kish says in one of the upstairs bedrooms. It was in fact Sarandon playing socialite Doris Duke in the HBO drama *Bernard and Doris*.

Old Westbury Gardens' small-screen appearances include *Gossip Girl*, *Royal Pains*, and *Sex and the City*. Acclaimed photographer Annie Leibovitz has also photographed on the grounds. Kish not only watches the results when each film gets released but also occasionally enjoys a side gig as a movie extra.

"Once in a while I get in the show," he said. Kish's past film credits include bits as a waiter in *Gossip Girl* and a fix-it man in *Bernard and Doris*.

"I always try to endear myself to the crew," he said. "But I always do it on my day off."

Movie shoots aside, Kish prefers if you don't call Old Westbury Gardens a museum. "It's a living, breathing entity," he said. "It's not like we're stuck in the past. This is a vibrant place."

Old Westbury Gardens celebrated its 50th anniversary open to the public in 2009. The site receives some 60,000 visitors a year. Special events including a dog show, antique car show, and Scottish games are popular annual attractions. Weekly events include live concert performances and any number of classes that offer lessons in tai chi, yoga, nature photography, and watercolor painting. Old Westbury Gardens also hosts young graduate student landscape designers from around the world. The students have come from as far away as Ireland, Brazil, and Indonesia.

Kish says the current success of Old Westbury Gardens relies on three attributes.

"This house is as nice a house as you'll see anywhere, the grounds are spectacular, and the events are unique," he said. "To have the ability to enjoy all three makes this place truly spectacular. So if you live on Long Island and don't have a backyard, this can be it. And if you do have a backyard, this can make it bigger. Make it your home away from home."

■■■■ INFO

Admission to Old Westbury Gardens (house and grounds access) costs $10 for adults, $8 for seniors (over 62), $5 for children 7 to 12, and is free for children 6 and under. Admission is free for members.

Old Westbury Gardens is open weekends Apr. through Dec.; and daily late Apr. through late Oct. (closed Tues.). Hours are 10 AM– 5 PM. Westbury House opens at 11 AM. Guided 45-minute tours of Westbury House are available daily every half hour. Guided garden tours are at 11 AM and 2 PM (except Sun., when the tours are held at 1 and 2 PM). Call 516-333-0048 or visit www.oldwestbury gardens.org.

■■■■ GETTING THERE

Old Westbury Gardens is at 71 Old Westbury Road. From the west, take the Long Island Expressway (I-495), the L.I.E., to exit 39 (Glen Cove Road). Turn right on Old Westbury Road and continue for half a mile. Look for the main entrance gate on your left.

The following roundup encompasses nearby Albertson, Williston Park, North Hills, Westbury, Carle Place, and Jericho. It's not your traditional grouping of Long Island towns, but they're all a 10-minute or less drive west, southwest, and east of the gardens.

■■■■ OUTSIDE

Clark Botanic Garden (193 I. U. Willets Road, Albertson; 516-484-2208; www.clarkbotanic.org). No prizes for size, this 12-acre garden delight gets the job done with a small but fine collection of native spring wildflowers and wetland, rock garden, and medicinal plants. It's adjacent to the LIRR Albertson train station and just a five-minute drive to Old Westbury Gardens. Perfect for a picnic lunch. Open daily spring through fall and weekdays during winter. Admission is by donation.

Christopher Morley Park (Searingtown Road in North Hills just north of the Long Island Expressway exit 36, Searingtown Road; 516-571-8113; www.nassau countyny.gov). Named after the accomplished writer Christopher Morley, this 98-acre park invites comparison between the ultra-luxurious Old Westbury Garden digs and Morley's very modest one-room writing studio, the Knothole.

Morley, who wrote more than 50 books as well as thousands of letters, poems, columns, and short stories, was also an original Book-of-the-Month Club editor. Morley did much of his writing in this studio, which he originally built on his Roslyn Estates property nearby. The Knothole was moved to its present site in 1966, and the park was eventually renamed in Morley's honor.

The simple Knothole structure features appropriate bookcases, a bunk bed, a fireplace, and an oh-so-modern one-piece preassembled "dymaxion" bathroom, which was designed in 1936 by Morley's friend, inventor Buckminster Fuller.

Christopher Morley Park sports activities include courts for basketball, handball, paddleball, and tennis, as well as a children's playground and picnic areas. Immensely popular with the locals is the nine-hole par-30 golf course, a swimming pool, and an ice-skating rink open daily Dec. through Mar.

Admission to the park is free. Fees apply for the pool ($10 nonresident adults), golf ($20 for nonresidents), and skating rink ($14 for nonresident adults). Leisure Pass (Nassau County residents) discounts apply.

▮▮▮▮ EAT

Deli on Rye (1008 Willis Avenue, Albertson; 516-621-2471). Strip malls are no stranger to Long Island—and this book (you've nothing to fear). The first two culinary stops are in the Waldbaum's shopping center in Albertson. Deli on Rye offers kosher fare such as succulent pastrami and corned-beef sand-wiches, robust Hebrew National all-beef franks, and chicken matzo-ball soup that will cure whatever ails you.

Vincent's Italian Restaurant (1004 Willis Avenue, Albertson; 516-621-7530). Just next door, Vincent's has been a fixture in the area since the 1970s (I played my first video game there as a teen—okay, it was Pong!). For pizza by the pie or slice and traditional Italian fare to stay or to go.

Cardinali Bakery (465 Westbury Avenue, Carle Place; 516-997-3193; www.cardinalibakery.com). For Italian culinary treats such as sweet pastries and cannolis, mouthwatering (and addictive) butter cookies, and rustic Italian breads and onion rolls. From Old Westbury Gardens, venture south along Old Westbury Road directly into Ellison Avenue, then turn right at Westbury Avenue.

Frank's Steaks (4 Jericho Turnpike, Jericho; 516-338-4595; www.frankssteaks.com). A steakhouse staple in the Jericho area for decades. Romanian skirt steak and prime rib are the popular carnivore favorites. Frank's is also known for seafood, sushi, and traditional steakhouse sides such as creamed spinach and Frank's potatoes with sautéed onions. Open daily for dinner and weekdays for lunch. From Old Westbury Gardens, venture east along Jericho Turnpike. There's another location in Rockville Centre (54 Lincoln Avenue; 516-536-1500).

▮▮▮▮ EAT WILLY PARK FOOD TOUR

From Albertson, make your way south along Willis Avenue to Williston Park (some of the locals still call it Willy Park) for a number of good dining and shopping options on Willis and Hillside avenues.

Riverbay Seafood Bar and Grill (700 Willis Avenue, Williston Park; 516-742-9191; www.riverbay restaurant.com). Your wallet won't walk away unscathed by the prices at this serious seafood restaurant, a Williston Park mainstay since 1980, but you should leave satisfied. A very popular Sunday brunch offers the essential omelet, waffle, and carving stations as well as raw bar and tasty seafood options. Open daily for dinner and weekdays for lunch.

Ceriello Fine Foods (541 Willis Avenue, Williston Park; 516-747-0277; www.ceriellofinefoods .com). Ceriello's offers authentic Italian gourmet delicacies to take home. My grade-school best friend's mom, Mrs. Ciccarella, used to make us walk *a whole mile* just to get sausage and cheese at Ceriello's. Ah, but that Sunday-afternoon meal couldn't be beat. Thanks, Mrs. Ciccarella!

Hildebrandt's (84 Hillside Avenue, Williston Park; 516-741-0608; www.hildebrandts.kp search.com). This neighborhood staple (since 1927) combines old-fashioned ice cream parlor, candy store, and vintage lunch-eonette with an updated menu of tasty affordable chicken and pasta dishes. Wash it all down with a smooth satisfying French ice cream soda.

Willy Parkers American Bar and Grill (71 Hillside Avenue, Williston Park; 516-750-8125; www.willyparkers.com). See that—folks around here really do call it Willy Park! A newcomer to the Hillside Avenue strip, Willy Parkers offers a generous menu of pub-style fare from chicken wings ($9) to burgers ($12) but then kicks it up a notch with select entrées such as hearty seafood paella of clams, mussels, shrimp, chorizo sausage, and saffron rice ($22). There's the tap to match with some 30 draft beers available. And for the sports fan fix, there are flat-screen TVs at every turn. Open daily for lunch, dinner, and late night.

Ivy Cottage (38 Hillside Avenue, Williston Park; 516-877-2343; www.kpsearch.com/df/ivy cottage). Excellent continental

American fare meets cozy cottage quaint. The crabmeat Napoleon is a good place to start, and the roasted Long Island duckling is a good place to continue. Open weekdays for lunch and daily for dinner.

■■■■ SHOP

Peter Andrews (46 Hillside Avenue, Williston Park; 516-742-1331, www.peterandrews.com). The local place for bed, bath, and tabletop. There's another location in Huntington (444 E. Jericho Turnpike; 631-424-0002) as well as a furniture warehouse in Farmingdale (160 Smith Street; 631-845-5512).

Hick's Nurseries (100 Jericho Turnpike, Westbury; 516-334-0066; www.hicksnursery.com). Green thumbs to the front of the line. Hick's has been around since 1853, making it Long Island's oldest nursery and gardening center. The space also offers an aquarium center, gardening workshops, tons of holiday decorations and decorating ideas, and visits from Santa—a Christmas tradition in these parts.

■■■■ AFTER DARK

Capital One Bank Theatre at Westbury (960 Brush Hollow Road, Westbury; 516-334-0800; order tickets through www.live nation.com). The Capital One Bank Theatre at Westbury is fondly remembered as the Westbury Music Fair. I recently went to a Genesis tribute band concert there and a Mineola High School reunion broke out—in the round! Pretty much every seat in the house is a good one. The venue features cover bands such as the Musical Box and contemporary crooners such as Tony Bennett and Melissa Etheridge. Leaving the parking lot after the show requires a bit of patience.

■■■■ SPECIAL EVENTS

April: **Dog Show** at Old Westbury Gardens.

May: **Spring Plant Sale** at Clark Botanic Gardens.

June: **Antique Car Show** at Old Westbury Gardens.

Summer: **English roses** at Old Westbury Gardens.

August: **Scottish Games** at Old Westbury Gardens.

December: **Holiday decorations** at Old Westbury Gardens.

■■■■ STAY

Holiday Inn Westbury (369 Old Country Road, Carle Place, 516-997-5000). Basic rooms that leave you close to Old Westbury Gardens as well as Roosevelt Field shopping (see Chapter 9). Rooms start at $189 per night and as low as $139 for fall rates booked in advance.

▪▪▪▪ ESTATES TO ESTATE SALES: ESTATE, GARAGE, AND TAG SALE TIPS

An estate sale is a garage sale is a tag sale? Not exactly. Whereas garage sale hosts schlep their unwanted treasures from the basement to the driveway for a weekend of wheeling and dealing, estate sales are often held inside the home of a recently dearly departed family member. Not only do you get to sneak about and see what the interior of the house looks like, usually everything is up for sale—and I mean EVERYTHING!—furniture, bric-a-brac, a half-used roll of aluminum foil, even the lighting fixtures off the ceiling. Many of these sales attract pros who buy at a discount and resell at a profit at their own antiques stores or on eBay. That translates to one of the following: you find a treasure, and it makes your day, or you've just ruined your morning dealing with a pushy rude lot who are after the same bargains as you. Here's how to make the task more enjoyable.

Find: Estate and garage sale listings are available at www.newsday.com. Others are also listed at craigslist.com.

Map: Choose a few sales in a given area and make a morning of it.

Get there early: For the best selection of goods or...

Get there late: The hosts are practically giving the stuff away by the end of the afternoon.

Be prepared: To sometimes wait in line to enter a house hosting an estate sale—that's how busy they can get. Some even admit by wristband only.

Bargain: Make them an offer they can't refuse.

Seal the deal: And walk away with a secondhand treasure at a good price.

If you can't make an estate sale, browse two floors of secondhand treasures at the **St. Vincent de Paul Society** thrift store (2160 Jericho Turnpike, Garden City Park; 516-746-8250).

▪▪▪▪ LIRR OPTIONS/ LOCAL TAXI INFO

Old Westbury Gardens is a 2-mile cab ride east along I.U. Willets Road from the Albertson Long Island Rail Road station (Oyster Bay branch). One-way fare costs about $11 through North Shore Plandome Taxi (516-747-5555). Access is also available from the

Westbury LIRR station (Port Jefferson branch) through Stuart's of Westbury Taxi (516-334-2900). About $6.50 for the one-way fare.

▮▮▮▮ FYI

Yours truly grew up in Albertson—hey, I've got to start with my hometown! I am a proud suburban boy at heart. What a great place to grow up with the most wonderful neighbors you'd ever meet!

▮▮▮▮ READS AND RESOURCES

Morley, who edited two editions of the highly regarded reference tome *Bartlett's Familiar Quotations,* was a man of many quotes himself. Here are two to live by:

"Read, every day, something no one else is reading. Think, every day, something no one else is thinking. Do, every day, something no one else would be silly enough to do. It is bad for the mind to continually be part of unanimity."

And:"No one appreciates the very special genius of your conversation as the dog does."

▮▮▮▮ NEXT STOP

Check out Chapter 9, which offers some suggested food options in nearby Mineola, mall-style shopping at Roosevelt Field, and, if the kids are in tow, a visit to Museum Row.

2 • MEDIEVAL MAGIC IN SANDS POINT: *Sands Point Preserve*

Sands Point, Port Washington, Manhasset, Kings Point, Great Neck

A 13th-century French-style manor house and a castle—or two—make the perfect backdrop for these modern medieval times.

Sands Point Preserve offers year-round grounds visits, hiking trails, and three of the finest examples of Gold Coast mansions you will ever see. The architecture will leave you breathless, and a visit around Labor Day weekend will set you back at least 500 years.

The architecture of note includes the magnificent Hempstead House, which was originally built by financier Howard Gould. In 1917 Gould then sold the property to Daniel and Florence Guggenheim. Today, the space is rented out to weddings and was recently used in the production of the short-lived NBC drama *Kings.*

The nearby Castle Gould is now used as museum space and administrative offices. It looks like an authentic castle, as it was designed to be reminiscent of Ireland's Kilkenny Castle.

Finally, the Falaise, from the French word meaning cliff—it

overlooks the Long Island Sound—was the home of Harry F. Guggenheim, the son of Daniel and Florence. Summer guided Falaise tours offer a peek into Harry's fascination with all things from medieval Europe. Harry Guggenheim traveled throughout Europe and gobbled up fragments of medieval houses, including an authentic 15th-century altar and a 16th-century Spanish writing desk. Paintings, statues, even entire staircases, were all purchased and imported to carry out the theme of European nobility.

In 1939, Harry Guggenheim married his third wife, Alicia Patterson. One year later, the pair started the Long Island newspaper *Newsday*. Patterson had to abide by a few rules when it came to the Falaise's design elements. The only two rooms she could have a hand in decorating were her bridge room and bedroom. Everything else was off-limits as Guggenheim wished to maintain the consistent feel and decor of an authentic Normandy manor. The pair lived in the house until

*Sands Point
Preserve
Hempstead
House*

their deaths (Patterson in 1963 and Guggenheim in 1971). The house was then transferred to Nassau County. The Falaise and its contents remain much the same as when Guggenheim died.

The entire 216-acre site makes a most fitting backdrop for the annual Medieval Fair, which has been held on the grounds for the past three decades. Kingdom of Acre member Mary Redler offers the first pointer of the day.

"This is not a Renaissance Fair," she said. "That came later, after the year 1500. The medieval times range from about 1000 to 1500."

So what's Redler's exact title? She says it depends on if you're referring to the corporate, kingdom, or territorial side of things. She handles much of the public relations for Medieval Scenarios and Recreations, Ltd., which oversees the corporate side of the Kingdom of Acre.

"But I'm also the steward of the territory Kyrenia, which takes up most of Long Island," she said.

She explains that modern medievalism has kingdoms divided up into geographical territories. The Kingdom of Acre boasts about 150 members who come mostly from Long Island, a.k.a. Kyrenia, and from as far away as upstate New York, Connecticut, and Maryland. Members get together about once a month for any number of activities, which include martial arts tournaments and period-crafts demonstrations. It's also a place to show off medieval fashion dos and don'ts.

Just don't call them costumes.

"We call it garb," Redler said. "Because if it was a costume, we'd be dressing up and pretending. We're not. We're trying to re-create the history."

Redler says Medieval Scenarios

and Recreations is chartered by New York State as an educational organization. The group offers historical reenactments and demonstrations to the likes of church groups and the Boy Scouts and at their annual Sands Point medieval bash. She adds that Castle Gould provides one of the best settings in which to hold a medieval festival.

"It's right out of the Middle Ages," she said.

The event, held two weekends every mid-September, offers a number of authentic medieval-era activities. The crowning—and kidnapping—of the queen and the resulting siege of the castle are popular crowd-pleasers. Other fest faves include armored fighting, fencing, and jousting, the most popular event of all. Medieval Fair master of ceremonies Michael Burkhardt, a.k.a. Sir Balin Devaliere, offers insight on the afternoon's games.

Burkhardt explains that professional jousters traveled throughout Europe going from joust to joust in order to make a living.

"Jousters were sons of nobility who had to somehow make it in the world," Burkhardt said. "They were the NASCAR of the day."

Burkhardt says the jousting circuit offered a variety of purses to win.

"But it was a hard way to make a living," he said. "It was very dangerous."

He says to consider that a jouster would be wearing 45 pounds of full-plated armor, riding a 1,600-pound horse, which he refers to as a "locomotive," all the while carrying a 9-foot oak lance. The festival re-creates all of the above.

"Imagine all that weight, that pressure, that force at the end of a 9-foot oak staff," he tells the audience. "If that hit you in the chest, you'd fly off that horse."

Medieval Fair jousters

With that, two riders gallop head-on in a jousting duel. One lance shatters upon contact with the other and wooden shards fly through the air, to the delight of the audience. The knights also demonstrate other equine games of skill, such as the spear throw, spinning quintain practice, and the full-gallop precision sword dissection of stationary apples and cabbages. The knights make medieval coleslaw of the ingredients at hand. These modern-day jousters consistently hit their mark again and again. It's actually quite impressive.

Burkhardt pokes polite fun and teases everyone from the jousters—"Look at that hair in the wind!"—to the audience, riling them at any moment's lull. As master of ceremonies/medieval-era wise guy, he keeps things moving briskly along.

"It's all good-natured. I just love getting the kids involved," he said. "I love to share my passion for those times. I love the Middle Ages."

■ ■ ■ ■ INFO

Grounds admission costs $5 per car; $2 per walk-in. Access is free on Wed. The Preserve is open Apr. through Dec. Hours are 9 AM–7:30 PM daily. Falaise tours cost $5 and are held Thurs. through Sun. at noon, 1, 2, and 3 PM early June through late Oct. No tours during the Medieval Fair weekends. Fair admission costs $10. Call 516-571-7900 or visit www.sandspoint preserve.org.

■ ■ ■ ■ GETTING THERE

Sands Point Preserve is at 127 Middle Neck Road in Port Washington. Take the L.I.E. to exit 36—Searingtown Road North. Continue for 6 miles. Searingtown Road eventually turns directly into Port Washington Boulevard and then Middle Neck Road.

■ ■ ■ ■ OUTSIDE

Leeds Pond Preserve (1526 North Plandome Road, Plandome Manor; 516-627-9400). This small 35-acre preserve offers winding trails, gorgeous views of Manhasset Bay, and a Victorian house, which is home to the Science Museum of Long Island (516-627-9400; www.smli.org), a living outdoor nature classroom for area schoolkids.

Saddle Rock Grist Mill (Grist Mill Lane, Saddle Rock adjacent to Great Neck; 516-571-7900). This tidal mill was once used to grind corn and grain. The mill is restored to the mid-1800s but was constructed around 1700. And talk about primitive but quite capable ingenuity—it still works! It's one of the few in the country that does. It's a quick free visit.

Open Sun. afternoons usually May through Oct.

▪▪▪▪ SIGHTSEE

Chrysler Estate (300 Steamboat Road, Kings Point; www.usmma .edu). Most Long Island estates have been transformed into museum space or incorporated into university campuses. The Walter P. Chrysler estate is one of the latter. Originally built as the home of milliner Henri Bendel around 1916, the estate now houses administrative offices for the U.S. Merchant Marine Academy. The campus also plays home to beautiful waterfront views as well as the **American Merchant Marine Museum** (516-773-5515). Situated in the campus' Barstow House, this small museum is big on nautical nostalgia, complete with navigational instruments, ship's models, and the ship's wheel from the USS *Constitution*. Open Tues. through Fri. 10 AM—3 PM and weekend afternoons. Closed in July.

▪▪▪▪ WATERFRONT

North Hempstead Beach Park (West Shore Road, Port Washington; 516-883-6074). As kids we spent a lot of time here. Until 2008 the space was divided into Bar Beach and Hempstead Harbor Park. Now unified, the area features a waterfront promenade,

fishing pier, boat ramp, and bathhouse. Activities include basketball and handball courts, horseshoe pits, and a playground as well as plenty of room for a weekend family reunion complete with sheltered picnic areas and barbecues. That said, the pricey $20 daily nonresident fee ($15 residents) may keep you away. Park closes at dark; fees collected daily in the summer season 9 AM— 5 PM.

▪▪▪▪ EAT PORT WASHINGTON

Frank's Pizzeria (14 Main Street, Port Washington; 516-883-9390). For a tasty pizza slice at very informal digs.

Amigos (52 Main Street, Port Washington; 516-883-1315). A very pleasant dining experience when Mexican is on your mind. For generous portions, friendly service, and reasonable prices (the recommended enchiladas amigos cost a bargain $11.50; most entrées $11—15). The marinade of choice for grilled platters: Dos Equis amber beer. Open daily for lunch and dinner. Near the LIRR train station.

Finn Mac Cool's (205 Main Street; Port Washington; 516-944-3439; www.finnmaccoolsny.com.) Finn's has been a Port Washington institution since 1984. The restaurant on one side, bar on the other serves up traditional Irish fare (bangers n' mash $16), pub-style appetizers, burgers ($11), and contemporary American cuisine (blackened chicken breast $12). The restaurant, popular with local families, is open daily for lunch and dinner.

Ayhan's Mediterranean Marketplace (293 Main Street, Port Washington; 516-767-1400; www.ayhans.com). Ayhan's offers three ways to please in Port Washington—and please the palate they do. **Ayhan's Fish-Kebab** (286 Main Street; 516-883-1515) offers excellent grilled whole fish dishes and specialty entrées reasonably priced ($14–20). **Ayhan's Shish-Kebab** (283 Main Street; 516-883-9309) offers succulent beef, chicken, and lamb kebabs and mixed grill fare (other locations may be found in Baldwin, Carle Place, Plainview, and Rockville Center). The Marketplace features fresh gourmet sandwiches, wraps, a "pick-your-own" lunch sold by the pound with dozens of selections, a bounty of packaged goods blessed by the Mediterranean sun, and cafeteria seating with harbor views. All open daily for lunch and dinner; Marketplace also serves breakfast.

La P'tite Framboise Bistro (294 Main Street, Port Washington; 516-767-7164; www.laptite framboise.com) The name of this bistro translates to "the little raspberry." This serious French restaurant offers traditional bistro fare at reasonable prices. Sample a croque monsieur ($9) open-face warm ham and cheese sandwich for lunch (a croque madame appropriately tops the creation with a fried egg); steak frites ($27) or coquilles St. Jacques ($25) for dinner; and crepes for Sunday brunch. Mussels marinières ($13), in Provençal or Pernod flavors, are available at every sitting.

Louie's Oyster Bar & Grille (395 Main Street, Port Washington; 516-883-4242; www.louiesoyster barandgrille.com). Another Port Washington institution (Louie's dates to 1905), the emphasis here is on good seafood with a beautiful harbor view. Menu choices of note include the Uptown Mac and Cheese with lobster, scallops, and shrimp smothered in Gouda, fontina, and Asiago cheeses ($22), and the Monday and Tuesday Clambake of soup or salad, two lobsters, mussels, clams, potato, corn, and dessert ($35).

Benihana (2105 Northern Boulevard, Manhasset; 516-627-3400; www.benihana.com). For dinner and a culinary show. One of the original Benihana grills. Open daily for lunch and dinner. Dinner $17–43.

Bryant & Cooper Steak House (2 Middle Neck Road; Roslyn; 516-627-7270; www.bryantandcooper .com). Quintessential steakhouse with all the fancy fixins: quality steaks, adventurous wine selection, polite atmosphere, and serious bill—the filet mignon costs $43.

■ ■ ■ ■ **SHOP**

Dolphin Book Store (941 Port Washington Boulevard, Port Washington; 516-767-2650). In a land of big box and Internet stores, it's always fun to browse—and buy—from a small independent bookstore.

Red Door Antiques (289 Main Street, Port Washington, 516-883-5125). This small shop offers fine antiques, fun collectibles, and the occasional kitschy knick-knack at reasonable prices.

Americana Manhasset (Northern Boulevard at Searingtown Road; www.americanamanhasset .com). As the vivacious and rich Karen Walker (Megan Mullally) of TV's *Will & Grace* fame once said: "shoulda, woulda, Prada." Better known as the Miracle Mile, the Americana shopping center offers upscale posh designer boutiques that include everything from Cartier to Juicy Couture, Fendi to Salvatore Ferragamo, and Versace to Van Cleef & Arpels. Go ahead. Save the economy. About 70 stores in all at Americana and a number of larger department stores also nearby along Northern Boulevard including Lord & Taylor.

■ ■ ■ ■ **SPECIAL EVENTS**

Late July: **Port Washington Antique Street Fair** along lower Main Street.

■ ■ ■ ■ **DRIVING TIPS**

Window of (photo) opportunity: private security shushes you along, but for beautiful Long Island Sound sunsets and a brief glimpse of the Manhattan skyline on clear nights, continue past the Sands Point Preserve (or exit right from the parking lot) to Lighthouse Road, which makes a half-circle back onto Middle Neck Road. Bring the camera for a quick but scenic shot. You'll know it when you see it.

■ ■ ■ ■ **STAY**

The Andrew Hotel (75 N. Station Plaza, Great Neck; 516-482-2900; www.andrewhotel.com). Boutique chic steps from the Great Neck LIRR train station. Rooms surprisingly reasonable for the area, starting at about $179 a night.

■ ■ ■ ■ **LIRR OPTIONS/ LOCAL TAXI INFO**

The Sands Point Preserve is about 2 miles north of the Port Washington train station (Port Washington branch). Delux Transportation Services (516-883-1900) offers cab service for about $8.

■ ■ ■ ■ FYI

A pause for paws. In its steadfast mission to care for our four-legged friends, the **North Shore Animal League** (25 Davis Avenue, Port Washington; 516-883-7575; www.nsalamerica.org) has adopted almost one million pets into loving homes since 1944.

The **U.S. Merchant Marine Academy** trains young midshipmen to become merchant mariners who wish to work in the commercial shipping industry. Although some small fees apply, tuition, room and board, books, and uniforms are free.

■ ■ ■ ■ READS AND RESOURCES

Long Island native Billy Joel's 1980 hit single "It's Still Rock & Roll to Me" references the area near the Manhasset shopping center mentioned above. In it Joel sings,

'What's the matter with the car I'm driving?'
   'Can't you tell that it's out of style?'
   'Should I get a set of whitewall tires?'
   'Are you gonna cruise the Miracle Mile?'

In Peace and War: A History of the U.S. Merchant Marine Academy by Jeffrey Cruikshank and Chloë Kline thoroughly chronicles the history of this important Long Island learning institution.

Read *We* by aviator Charles Lindbergh. Handwritten framed pages of the text adorn the walls of the Falaise house at Sands Point Preserve. Lindbergh was often a guest of Falaise owner Harry F. Guggenheim and wrote the book on the premises.

Visit the **Town of North Hempstead** at www.northhempstead.com.

■ ■ ■ ■ NEXT STOP

A little art with your estate visit? Check out the Nassau County Museum of Art in the next chapter.

3 • THE ART OUTDOORS IN ROSLYN: *Nassau County Museum of Art*

Roslyn, Roslyn Harbor, Sea Cliff, Glen Cove

Many Gold Coast mansions are indeed works of art in their own right, but the Frick Estate in Roslyn goes one artistic step further.

The estate was the previous home of Childs Frick, whose dad bought him the digs as a wedding present. Frick and his bride lived at the Roslyn residence for some five decades. The estate, dubbed Clayton, was acquired by Nassau County in the late 1960s, a few years after Frick's death. Opened in 1989 as the Nassau County Museum of Art, the space now houses ongoing temporary art exhibits, a MiniArt Museum geared for children, and dozens of outdoor sculptures. It has become Nassau County's—if not Long Island's—premier space for exhibition art.

The temporary exhibitions come and go—the museum has highlighted luminaries from Norman Rockwell to Andy Warhol and representatives of all artistic movements in between—but it is the grand, sometimes abstract, but always intriguing outdoor art that has stood the test of time. There are a number of styles that make for a great outdoor sculpture, says acting director Constance Schwartz.

"You have a style that appears to have come from the building age, the industrial age," she said. She notes the works of artists Mark diSuvero and Richard Serra.

"These works are hard-edge monuments that soar to the sky," Schwartz said. "But they still complement nature."

Schwartz then cites sculptures she calls organic.

"These are perhaps more abstract," she said. "They're full of flowing lines that remind you of life. They have a more personal kind of expression. And they look completely different when placed against the landscape."

She references artist Niki de Saint Phalle's *Snake Tree,* a 30-foot-tall brilliantly colored mirrored mosaic that sprouts from the ground like a tree trunk with multiple snake heads.

"It's just wonderful," she said. "The children go crazy for this one."

Taking a more realistic approach is Fernando Botero's "Man on Horseback," a cherub caricature of a man sitting atop an equally rounded horse.

"Each of these styles portrays a different vocabulary, a different kind of moment as it's placed against nature," Schwartz said.

It is indeed that natural backdrop that makes for a most unique outdoor gallery. Schwartz says the Nassau County Museum of Arts possesses a simple but extraordinary quality.

"And that is we have 145 gorgeous acres of property," she said. "So we have the wherewithal to be able to showcase these sculptures in a different light than through an interior space. And that gives the piece an entirely different life of its own."

It's true. You take a stroll near the small pond and don't expect to see the likes of Allen Bertoldi's *Wood Duck*. The piece has nothing to do with a feathered friend and instead portrays itself as a massive black steel circle that "floats" on the tranquil waterline. The visitor is equally drawn to the likes of Alejandro Colunga's multipiece *Chair, House for Doves,* which appears as if some abstract aliens have landed and decided to stay put.

"We get so many visitors who just walk the grounds—the casual visitor, a school group, a businessperson on a lunch break," Schwartz said. "They come to relax, take photos, write about the sculptures they see. It's so special to see somebody not only sitting next to a tree, but sitting next a sculpture eating a sandwich, reading a book, enjoying their day. That lifeline to the sculpture is so special."

Nassau County Museum of Art wood duck

Nassau County Museum of Art

Schwartz takes a stroll as often as possible to remind herself of where she is.

"I'm very happy when I can put my nose out the door. The thing I particularly love to do is walk the formal gardens," she said. "The azalea garden has this beautiful sculpture by Charles Rumsey called *The Three Graces*. It's wonderfully reminiscent of the turn of the century."

The Nassau County Museum of Art celebrated its 20th anniversary in 2009. In all 52 sculptures presently grace the outdoor grounds. Schwartz is so right when she says that each sculpture sends a different artistic message.

My favorite on the site is Bertoldi's *Redbank 31—Nassau Variation*. Here, 16 separate rectangular steel portals stretch a distance of some 30 feet. They are placed in a way as if to induce an infinite optical illusion. When I was a youngster in my twenties, my friends and I hopscotched our way through these metal doors. Upon my recent return, the work spoke to me like an old forgotten friend— perhaps a time line of my life. I've passed through some of those portals. And I'm glad I got to pass through a few more now. I'll happily save a few of those doors for future visits. It made me serenely content to revisit this wonderful artistic walk in the woods.

■■■■ INFO

Access to the grounds of the Nassau County Museum of Arts is free. (How's that for a bargain? There's only a $2 parking fee per car on weekends.) Admission to the Arnold and Joan Saltzman Fine Art Building (the main building that hosts the exhibitions) costs about $10 for adults, $8 for seniors, and $4 for students and children (4–12). MiniArt Museum visits cost $5 for adults and $4 for seniors, students, and children.

Main building hours are Tues. through Sun. 11 AM–4:45 PM. The MiniArt Museum for Children is open Tues. through Sun. 12–4:30 PM. Exhibition tours are daily at 2 PM; mansion tours are held Sat. at 1 PM.

■■■■ GETTING THERE

The Nassau County Museum of Art is at 1 Museum Drive in Roslyn Harbor just off Northern Boulevard (Route 25A), 1/4-mile west of Glen Cove Road. Take the L.I.E. to exit 39, Glen Cove Road. Drive north to Route 25A and turn left. Look for the sign on your right.

■■■■ OUTSIDE

Roslyn Pond Park (Main Street and Paper Mill Road, Roslyn). Now known as Gerry Park, but more affectionately known as the Roslyn Duck Pond, this small park provides a relaxing spot for an afternoon stroll. The park is home to the replica Onderdonk-Remsen-Gaine Paper Mill, the original of which dates to 1773.

Bailey Arboretum (294 Bayville Road at the corner of Feeks Lane, Lattingtown; 516-570-8020; www .baileyarboretum.org). A small North Shore respite of 43 acres, the Bailey Arboretum is home to well-marked trails, tranquil ponds, perennial gardens, and a number of dawn redwoods. You can bring a picnic, and you can also bring the dog. Open year-round daily 9 AM—4 PM. Admission is free.

▪▪▪▪ SIGHTSEE

Cedarmere Estates (Bryant Avenue in Roslyn Harbor; 516-571-8130). Just east of the art museum and north of Roslyn Village you'll find Cedermere Estates, the former home of the poet and journalist William Cullen Bryant. The space shares the land of the Frick estate mentioned above. The landscape was designed by Frederick Law Olmsted of Central Park fame. Cedarmere is open weekends May through early Nov.

▪▪▪▪ WATERFRONT

Garvies Point Museum and Preserve (50 Barry Drive, Glen Cove; 516-571-8010; www.garviespoint museum.com). In like flint. Venture west then north from the Frick Estate to find a seaside spot that explores local geology and Native American archaeology. Arrowheads, Indian paint pots, and flint stones all present and accounted for. Admission costs about $3 for adults. Closed Sun. and Mon.

Morgan Memorial Park Beach (at the end of Landing Road on Germaine Street, Glen Cove; 516-676-3766). Adjacent to Garvies Point, Morgan Beach offers beautiful Long Island Sound views and a short hiking trail. That said, it's only open to residents during summer daytime hours. The solution: plan your visit for an after-dinner evening stroll.

▪▪▪▪ EAT

The Chalet Restaurant & Tap Room (1 Railroad Avenue, Roslyn; 516-621-7975; www.roslynchalet .com). Steps from the Roslyn LIRR train station, the Chalet has been a mainstay in these parts for decades but recently enjoyed an ultramod makeover. In keeping with the swanky casual pub scene, stick with the fun tapas and appetizer menu such as slider burgers with pepper jack cheese and tomato salsa ($4), crispy shrimp fritters ($4), and cheese fondue ($4), all perfect to share. VIP room and fancy martinis, too. Open daily for dinner and later Fri. and Sat. nights.

Taproom open until 4 AM.

K.C. Gallagher's Pub (325 Sea Cliff Avenue, Sea Cliff; 516-656-0996). A local cozy joint with the characters to match. Good pub fare at reasonable prices.

■■■■ EAT GLEN COVE FOOD TOUR

Wild Fig (167 Glen Street, Glen Cove; 516-656-5645; wildfig online.com). For authentic Eastern Mediterranean and Turkish specialties. Try their signature brick-oven pides—think a sauceless oval pizza garnished with a variety of tasty toppings such as grilled eggplant, tomato, garlic, and Kashar cheese ($9). Also in Syosset (631 Jericho Turnpike; 516-558-7744) and Garden City (829 Franklin Avenue; 516-739-1002).

Razzano's (286 Glen Street, Glen Cove; 516-676-3745; www.razzanos.com). My (Italian) hero. Razzano's is a wonderful imported Italian delicacies store, but go there for the incredibly fresh gourmet sandwiches, such as the Roma stuffed with prosciutto, mozzarella, sliced eggplant, and roasted peppers. Hero sizes range from 1- to 7-footers. Equally fresh and tasty salads and accompaniments as well.

Marra's (1 School Street, Glen Cove; 516-609-3335; www.marras online.com). If you prefer to stay awhile Italian-style, give Marra's a try for traditional casual Italian fare that's very popular with the locals. The sausage dumplings appetizer with stir-fried broccoli rabe ($10) is a good way to begin any Marra's meal. Open daily for lunch and dinner.

The Polish Deli (18 Forest Avenue, Glen Cove; 516-277-1469; www.thepolishdeli.com). For cherry and cheese babkas, paczki (Polish jelly doughnuts), spot-on homemade pierogi (delivered to your door!), and imported Polish and European market foods such as canned goods, cookies, and cheeses. Open daily.

Steamboat Landing 76 Shore Road, Glen Cove; 516-759-3921). For casual seafood and American fare. Outdoor seating come summer and live music all year round.

■■■■ SHOP

Rose's General Store (327 Sea Cliff Avenue, Sea Cliff; 516-277-1044). For fine linen and lace, Americana and antiques, and wooden and wind-up toys.

Dreams East (359 Sea Cliff Avenue, Sea Cliff; 516-656-4790; www.dreamseast.com). For the likes of candles, chimes, stained glass, soaps, incense, and inspirational items.

Charles of Glen Cove (19 Glen Street, Glen Cove; 516-671-3111) Old-school hardware and housewares.

■ ■ ■ ■ SPECIAL EVENTS

July and August Weekends: **Morgan Park Summer Music Festival Series** (516-671-0017; www.morgan parkmusic.org).

Early October: Sea Cliff Avenue and vicinity plays home to grand Victorian houses and annual **Sea Cliff Mini-Mart**, a popular street fair of some 200 vendors offering handmade crafts and food kiosks.

■ ■ ■ ■ AFTER DARK

Roslyn Cinemas (20 Tower Street, Roslyn; 516-621-8488; www.clear viewcinemas.com). The non-megaplex way to enjoy a first-run or art-house flick in Roslyn.

Ballroom Legacy (185A Glen Cove Avenue, Sea Cliff; 516-609-3269; www.ballroomlegacy.com). Ballroom and Latin dance studio. Most dance classes held weekday evenings and Sat. afternoons.

■ ■ ■ ■ STAY

Roslyn Claremont Hotel (1221 Old Northern Boulevard, Roslyn; 516-625-2700; www.roslynclaremont hotel.com). Rooms start at $190.

■ ■ ■ ■ LIRR OPTIONS/ LOCAL TAXI INFO

The Nassau County Museum of Art is accessible from the Roslyn LIRR train station (Oyster Bay branch). Delux Transportation (516-621-4500) charges about $6.50 for the one-way fare for one person.

■ ■ ■ ■ FYI

Did George Washington really sleep here? Well, he did tour Long Island in 1790, and Roslyn was indeed one of his stops. Roslyn Village dates to the 1640s and is considered one of the oldest settled towns on Long Island (although the Roslyn name didn't stick until the 1840s). Washington visited Hendrick Onderdonk, who built the paper mill in Roslyn Duck Pond mentioned above.

■ ■ ■ ■ READS AND RESOURCES

Robin Williams and film crew shut down the town when shooting *The World According to Garp* in the early 1980s. In the film, Williams walks past the movie theater mentioned above to admire his character's book in the shop window next door.

Visit the **City of Glen Cove** at www.glencove-li.com.

Visit the **Village of Sea Cliff** at www.seacliff-ny.gov.

Visit the **Roslyn Landmarks Society** at www.roslynlandmarks .org.

Visit the **Village of Roslyn** at www.historicroslyn.org.

■ ■ ■ ■ NEXT STOP

The South Shore boasts its own great estates. Have a look at Chapter 16.

4 • A PRESIDENTIAL PALACE IN OYSTER BAY: *Sagamore Hill*

Oyster Bay, Cove Neck, Locust Valley, Brookville, Bayville

Oyster Bay and neighboring Cove Neck hail to the chief and host Sagamore Hill, the estate home of Theodore Roosevelt, the 26th president of the United States. The National Park Service site offers lighthearted nonscripted tours that cover a variety of T.R. topics from family history, early 20th-century life, and the site of Sagamore Hill as the first Summer White House. Charles Markis, Chief of Interpretation, leads the tour.

Roosevelt was born in New York City and first summered in Cove Neck in the 1870s. His childhood nickname was Teedie; it was his first wife, Alice Lee, who called him Teddy. But Alice and his mother, Mittie, died hours apart in the same house on the same day—Valentine's Day 1884. Mittie died of typhoid and Alice died of Bright's disease due to complications from childbirth.

"He was devastated," Markis said. "He never used the name Teddy again."

Markis adds that the Teddy nickname was used more by the press and with mention of the iconic Teddy Bear.

"But his family always called him Theodore," Markis said. "We say T.R."

When his grandfather Cornelius died in 1871, Roosevelt inherited a small fortune to the tune of about $9 million—a tidy sum even by today's standards. Roosevelt then purchased Sagamore Hill in 1880 and six adjoining properties, which were all owned by relatives.

"It was like a big compound," Markis said. "And all of the families had children."

Having lots of children around was something Roosevelt enjoyed immensely. On any given day, the site played home to six of Roosevelt's children as well as another 16 cousins. Unlike other estates in the area that changed ownership many times, Sagamore Hill transferred directly from family residence to museum.

"And it's never been renovated," Markis said. "It's about 95 percent original."

T.R. lived there until his death in 1919, and his second wife, Edith, lived there until her death in 1948.

T.R.'s White House years between 1902 and 1908 marked

the first time a sitting president moved the seat of power from Washington, D.C., for an extended period of time.

"T.R. set this precedent," Markis said. "Now the head of state is followed by his staff."

As for the press corps, let's just say that way back when there was no such thing as a 24-hour news cycle.

"When T.R. first came here as president, the only phone in town was at Snouders Drug Store. So if the president got a phone call, Snouders' son would bicycle out to deliver the message."

T.R. in turn would make his way to the pharmacy to return the most dire of calls. The store still stands in downtown Oyster Bay today. Markis adds that when Sagamore Hill did get phone service, the extension was placed in the butler's pantry. Also in the pantry was the refrigerator-sized safe, which stored, among other things, the family silver and T.R.'s Nobel Peace Price, which he won in 1906. Of all the nearby Gold Coast estates, Markis says this was the most modest.

"This was a farm. It was the family home, the only one they had."

And it was decorated in typical T.R. style, down to the animal trophies, skin rugs, and deer antlers. The North Room, where T.R. met visiting dignitaries, is adorned with the likes of a buffalo head, an elephant foot–shaped waste basket, a rhino inkwell, and even his Rough Rider hat and saber.

"It was a room designed to impress," Markis said.

It's also a room that could make any present-day PETA visitor incensed—and it has.

"I wish I had been warned," a visitor once commented.

Consider yourself warned. Also consider this was the tradition of the day.

Sagamore Hill

Snouders Drug Store in Oyster Bay

But live critters were cared for as well. T.R. was known for his conservation efforts and was also an avid bird-watcher. He even once had the delicate duty of caring for the family pet guinea pig, which he conveniently kept tucked away in a White House desk drawer.

Besides the abundance of natural history treasures, a number of exquisite furnishings, such as intricately carved Herter Brothers cabinets, adorn the premises.

"And the occasional pieces from the Montgomery Ward or Sears catalog," said Markis.

T.R.'s study/library welcomes visitors with period furnishings and stacks of leather-bound books, and guests are also greeted by a wall of portrait photographs of the heroes whom T.R. admired most: Abraham Lincoln, his father Theodore Roosevelt Sr., Ulysses S. Grant, Chief Justice John Marshall, and George Washington. T.R. looked to the past for personal inspiration, but he also looked toward the future in the eyes of a child.

"Typically T.R. quit his day at four in the afternoon," Markis said. "Even if he was meeting with congressmen, senators, or ministers, there was a more important appointment he had to keep. And these visitors were often surprised to see T.R. playing with his children on the lawn."

With Sagamore Hill hosting some 6,000 schoolchildren a year on student field trips, that's an afternoon party T.R. would have undoubtedly loved.

■ ■ ■ ■ INFO

Tours cost $5. Site access includes entrance to the Theodore Roosevelt Museum (at Old Orchard), which is located on the premises. Call 516-922-4788 or visit www.nps.gov/sahi.

Markus says if you're if planning a weekend visit, arrive in the morning, because guided tours are offered on a first-come, first-served basis and sell out by early afternoon. Reservations are only accepted for groups.

■■■■ GETTING THERE

At 12 Sagamore Hill Road in Oyster Bay. Take the Northern State Parkway to exit 35N or the L.I.E. to exit 41N. Then take Route 106 north for 6 miles into Oyster Bay and turn right onto East Main Street and travel 2 miles. Turn left onto Cove Neck Road and drive 1.5 miles to Sagamore Hill (there are plenty of signs along the way).

■■■■ MORE STATELY VISITS

Planting Fields Arboretum State Historic Park (1395 Planting Fields Road, Oyster Bay; 516-922-9200, www.plantingfields.org). The nearby Coe Estate at the Planting Fields shows a fine comparison to the Roosevelt residence in a more opulent Tudor revival—style of luxury digs. The 409-acre plot of land includes formal gardens, an abundant greenhouse collection, and the 65-room Coe Hall. A visit is worthy of a stroll through all four seasons.

The greenhouse collection includes orchids, cacti, begonias, palms, and ferns as well as seasonal displays of Easter lilies, chrysanthemums, and poinsettias. A greenhouse visit is particularly welcome during inclement and winter weather—it's sure to lift your spirits. The greenhouse is open year-round.

Coe Hall tours are available spring through fall. A $6 parking fee is charged May through Oct. 31 and weekends and holidays from Nov. through Apr. 30. Coe Hall tours cost $3.50. The garden gift shop is worth a browse as well.

■■■■ OUTSIDE

Hoffman Center Nature Preserve and Wildlife Sanctuary (6000 Northern Boulevard, East Norwich; 516-922-3290; www.hoffman center.org). Who-hoo-hoo-hoo-hoo goes there? Take a guided evening stroll in search of some fine feathered Great Horned and Eastern Screech Owl friends. These Owl Prowls are led by the Theodore Roosevelt Sanctuary and Audubon Center fall through spring (about $10; reservations required). The 155-acre site also offers free guided nature walks the first and third Sat. of the month, Brewster Estate visits, and a Nature Photography Academy.

Humes Japanese Stroll Garden (347 Oyster Bay Road and Dogwood Lane, Locust Valley; 516-676-4486). Moments of Zen. Follow my haiku: Lift your summer soul. Seven-buck tranquility.

With pebbles, bamboo.

Okay, and another (I haven't done these since grade school!): Add a guided tour. And a tea ceremony. For five dollars more.

The Japanese Stroll Garden offers seasonal inner affirmations amid 4 acres of serenity late Apr. through Oct. The garden visit costs $7; tea ceremony costs $12 (reservations required for tea ceremony).

Bayville Adventure Park (8 Bayville Avenue, Bayville; 516-624-7433; www.bayvilleadventure park.com). The seaside Bayville Adventure Park can be summed up in three words: fun mini putt. Come fall, the name changes to the Bayville Screampark, which can also be summed up in three words: scary haunted house. This one's for the kids. Open daily in summer. The pirate adventure—themed mini putt costs about $10.

▪▪▪▪ WATERFRONT

Theodore Roosevelt Park is a small green space adjacent to the LIRR Oyster Bay train station. It's a great place for a casual picnic. The nearby dock makes for a great photo op.

The WaterFront Center (1 West End Avenue, Oyster Bay; 516-922-7245; www.thewaterfrontcenter .org). All hands on deck! This maritime education center provides a variety of nautical adventures including sailboat and kayak lessons and rentals as well as public sails aboard the *Christeen* oyster sloop May through early Nov. Two-hour sunset and fall foliage sails cost about $30.

▪▪▪▪ EAT OYSTER BAY

Oyster Bay Fish & Clam (103 Pine Hollow Road/Route 106, Oyster Bay; 516-922-5522). Here you'll find all the seafood staples and then some in a casual colorful atmosphere chock-full of Long Island, maritime, and bar memorabilia. Traditional seafood plates cost $25 and up; seafood pasta dishes $21 and up. No credit cards. Open daily.

Ralph's (117 Pine Hollow Road/ Route 106, Oyster Bay; 516-922-7257; www.ralphsices.com). It's a good time to mention the Ralph's Famous Italian Ices franchise chain. Authentic Italian ices, sherbet, and ice cream.

Canterbury's Oyster Bar & Grill (46 Audrey Avenue, Oyster Bay; 516-922-3614; www.canter buryalesrestaurant.com). The T.R.-inspired theme for this casual neighborhood bistro is "Speak softly and carry a big…steak." For steaks, seafood, salads, sandwiches, and wild game dishes. Dinner and pasta entrées start at about $16. Open daily.

BayKery Café (124 South Street, Oyster Bay; 516-922-7002). A good way to start the day. For breakfast (served all day); soup, salad, chili, and quiche for lunch; and sweet treats to stay or go.

Wild Honey (1 East Main Street, Oyster Bay; 516-922-4690; www.wildhoneyrestaurant.com). Inventive American cuisine in a rustic setting. Start with the crispy calamari ($10) that comes with a tangy Thai barbecue sauce and pickled Asian vegetables and continue with the fall-off-the-bone slow-cooked baby back ribs ($24) with luscious sweet potato hash. Open for lunch Tues. through Fri.; daily for dinner.

■ ■ ■ ■ SHOP

Buckingham Variety Store (36 Audrey Avenue, Oyster Bay; 516-922-4822; www.buckinghamvarietystore.com). Buckingham offers old school-style five-and-dime shopping and browsing for everything from T.R. T-shirts and coffee mugs to seaside-themed souvenirs and even those hard-to-find sewing notions that you've been looking for.

Chalikian (103 Audrey Avenue, Oyster Bay; 516-922-7222). It's time to visit Chalikian, which offers a cornucopia of antique clocks—from cuckoo to grandfather—as well as pocket watches and music boxes sold and repaired by Jacques Chalikian, a fourth-generation clockmaker.

Coin Galleries of Oyster Bay

(90 South Street/Route 106, Oyster Bay; 516-922-0222; www.rarecoingalleries.com). Numismatists to the front of the line. Other locations in Lynbrook and Levittown. Closed Sun.

Nobman's Hardware (14 East Main Street, Oyster Bay; 516-922-6233; www.nobmanshardware.com). This old-fashioned hardware store, which has been around since 1910 (I wonder if T.R. ever stopped by?), kicks it up a notch with the likes of attractive home furnishings, weather vanes, ship models, even kites for the kids. Their loyal local customer base even prompts a Web site section titled "Surviving Home Depot."

■ ■ ■ ■ SPECIAL EVENTS

Mid-October: Aw, shucks. Exactly what kind of festival does Oyster Bay celebrate annually? You get one guess. The annual **Oyster Festival** (516-628-1625; www.theoysterfestival.org) has been praising the marine mollusk since 1983 (it actually began as a tribute to T.R., who had a fondness for oysters, says the Web site). Held mid-Oct., events are situated along Audrey Avenue, Oyster Bay's main street, and at the waterfront Theodore Roosevelt Park. The fest features 30 food vendors, arts and crafts wares of 125 artisans, tall ships, street performers, live entertainment, and of course, oyster eating and shucking contests.

▪▪▪▪ AFTER DARK

The Tilles Center for the Performing Arts (720 Northern Boulevard, Brookville; 516-299-3100; www.tillescenter.org) presents an impressive variety of music, dance, and theater performances at the C. W. Post campus of Long Island University.

▪▪▪▪ STAY

East Norwich Inn (6321 Northern Boulevard East Norwich; 516-922-1500; www.eastnorwichinn.com). Rooms start at about $140 a night.

▪▪▪▪ LIRR OPTIONS/ LOCAL TAXI INFO

T.R often traveled to Oyster Bay via the Long Island Road—you can, too. Nearby LIRR stations include Oyster Bay (Oyster Bay branch) or Syosset (Huntington branch). To cab it to Sagamore Hill, call Oyster Rides (516-624-8294)—about $12 for the one-way fare per person; or Syosset Taxi (516-921-2141)—$12 for the fare.

▪▪▪▪ FYI

Oyster fun fact no. 1—When's the best time to eat oysters in season? The culinary rule of thumb used to be any month that contains the letter "r" (September through April). Not exactly. You can eat oysters year-round; they just taste better when the water is really cold.

Oyster fun fact no. 2—Similar to TV character Archie Bunker's pronunciation, some older generation New Yorkers, specifically Queens residents (such as my grandma Maggie), pronounced oyster as "erster." The same went for other "oi"-sound-containing words such as "terlit" for toilet and "berler" for boiler.

▪▪▪▪ READS AND RESOURCES

The Wilderness Warrior: Theodore Roosevelt's Crusade for America by presidential biographer Douglas Brinkley chronicles Roosevelt's national conservation legacy.

The Two Mrs. Grenvilles by Dominick Dunne is an old-money tale based on the life—and death—of William "Billy" Woodward, Jr., heir to the Hanover Bank fortune, and his tumultuous marriage to Ann Crowell, who accidentally shot her husband in their Oyster Bay estate in 1955 thinking he was an intruder. It's a juicy good read.

Visit the **Oyster Bay Chamber of Commerce** at www.visitoyster bay.com.

▪▪▪▪ NEXT STOP

Take in dinner and a movie in nearby Huntington (Chapter 6).

5 • STAR POWER IN CENTERPORT:
Vanderbilt Museum and Planetarium

Northport, Centerport, Kings Park, Smithtown

Nassau County doesn't get all the Gold Coast glory when it comes to Long Island's great estates. They made their way east into Suffolk County as well. Perhaps the most prominent is the Vanderbilt estate, which now houses a modest mansion, a natural history collection museum, and Long Island's largest planetarium. Affable guide Jim Ryan conducts a very animated tour.

Ryan explains that the estate was the summer home of William Kissam Vanderbilt II, an heir to the Vanderbilt family fortune.

"His was all inherited money," Hunt said. "He wasn't one of the Vanderbilts who made the money, he was one in the family line who got to enjoy the fortune."

We should all be so lucky.

Hunt explains that the money came from great-granddad Cornelius' shipping and railroad lines.

"When William was born in 1878, the Vanderbilts were the richest family in America," Hunt said.

Although "Willie K" was accepted into Harvard, he wasn't the school-going type. He dropped out of university, got married, and eventually built Eagle's Nest, his mansion on his 43-acre Centerport estate.

"He had the great combination of having a lot of time and a lot of money," Hunt said.

Vanderbilt purchased the land for one main reason, Hunt adds.

"And it's just on the other side of this archway," Hunt said as the tour group stands in the central courtyard. "Take a look."

Visible through the narrow archway is a stunning view of the tranquil blue Centerport Bay. Just past the protected inlet lies the Long Island Sound and, on the horizon, Stamford, Connecticut.

"This is the deepest sheltered bay on the northern shore of Long Island," Hunt said. "And he bought this property so he'd have a place to park his yachts."

Yes. Yachts. As in plural. "He owned 10 yachts in the course of his lifetime," Hunt said. "And the older he got the bigger they got."

Besides being an avid seafarer, Vanderbilt was also a car-racing enthusiast. He founded the Vanderbilt Cup Race in 1904, the first auto race in America. The race was first held on public roads in Nassau County and the $1,000 prize attracted competitors from all over the world. After a few successful years of races, the powers that be in Nassau County said no more races on public roads.

"So he built his own road," Hunt said. "He bought a 20-foot swath of land 48 miles long from Flushing to Ronkonkoma. It would become the Vanderbilt Motor Parkway."

Hunt says that the first race held on the Vanderbilt Motor Parkway in 1908 attracted 500,000 spectators. By 1910, some 750,000 people showed up.

"It was the Super Bowl of its day," Hunt said.

Unfortunately, when three spectators were killed near the finish line, New York state officials put an end to the race.

After a failed marriage and a tidy inheritance of more than $20 million after the death of his father in 1920, Vanderbilt spent most of his time traveling the world aboard his 285-foot luxury yacht, *Alva*, which came complete with a seaplane. Along the way, Vanderbilt amassed a fine collection of artifacts and natural history specimens. He was also a popular host when he stayed put in the Centerport mansion. Famous guests included Charles Lindbergh, Sonja Henie, Douglas Fairbanks, Jr., Fiorello La Guardia, George Gershwin, Henry Ford, President Franklin Roosevelt, and the Duke and Duchess of Windsor.

At the time of Vanderbilt's death in 1944, Hunt says the estate was valued at $36 million. The government took a whopping $30 million in estate taxes for

The Shack

Vanderbilt Estate

their own coffers; the rest of the money went to his heirs and as an endowment for the estate.

"It just goes to show that even the greatest American fortunes run their course," Hunt said.

The estate changed hands to Suffolk County in 1947. In the 1960s during the advent of the space race, the county was shopping around for a place to host a planetarium. They found their home at the Vanderbilt estate. The Vanderbilt Planetarium officially opened in 1971.

"Mr. Vanderbilt always envisioned the space as a museum open to the public," said Vanderbilt Museum Executive Director Carol Ghiorsi Hart.

Ghiorsi Hart says that Vanderbilt's love of exploration fits right into the Vanderbilt Museum mandate.

"He had the opportunity to travel all around the world several times," she said. "He also realized that many Long Islanders would never get that chance, so he wanted to bring a little bit of that world to the people of Long Island."

Ghiorsi Hart adds that the museum aspect is one way the Vanderbilt estate differs from other Gold Coast mansions. She says the galleries were installed during the 1920s and 1930s, when Vanderbilt was still alive.

"The museums were not an afterthought," Ghiorsi Hart said. "He hired the best designers, scientists, and academics that money could buy and built the marine and natural history museums on the grounds. He wanted to leave a legacy behind."

Ghiorsi Hart adds the planetarium fits right in.

"The family made all their money in transportation, and Vanderbilt was always interested in boats, cars, and planes. He would have definitely been interested in the space program," she said. "He was a speed demon, a man of adventure and excitement. He would have probably hitched a ride to outer space if he could. And he would have loved having the planetarium here."

▋▋▋▋ INFO

Mansion, grounds, and galleries access costs $7 for adults, $6 for students and seniors, and $3 for children (under 12). For mansion tour or planetarium show, add $5 for adults, $4 for students and seniors, and $3 for children under 12.

Site access for grounds and mansion are Tues. through Sat. 10 AM–5 PM. Sun. hours are 12–5 PM. Planetarium admission and hours listed below. Call 631-854-5555 or visit www.vanderbiltmuseum.org.

■ ■ ■ ■ GETTING THERE

The Vanderbilt Museum is at 180 Little Neck Road in Centerport. From the L.I.E. take exit 51N; from the Northern State Parkway take exit 42N, and from the Southern State Parkway take exit 39N.

Drive north on Deer Park Avenue and bear left at the fork (at the traffic light) onto Park Avenue. At the third light turn right onto Broadway and continue for about 5 miles until Route 25A. After crossing 25A you are now on Little Neck Road. The museum is a mile and a half on your right.

■ ■ ■ ■ AFTER DARK

The **Vanderbilt Planetarium** opened in 1971 as a way to boost interest in Vanderbilt estate visits. It's the largest planetarium facility on Long Island. Its domed 60-foot, 238-seat Sky Theater hosts original multimedia explorations of space for budding astronomers of all ages.

And then there are the laser shows, another popular planetarium staple. It's a trippy good time complete with music provided by the Beatles, Pink Floyd, U2, and Led Zeppelin. Any planetarium show makes for a fun date night.

The shows are held during regular operating hours on the hour and Thurs., Fri., and Sat. evenings and nights. Night sky observation sessions are open to the public Fri. nights, weather permitting, 9–11 PM.

Evening planetarium show and observatory fees are $7 for adults, $6 for students and seniors, and $3.50 for children. Evening laser show costs $10 for adults, $9 for students and seniors, and $8 for children. Observing is free with the purchase of a planetarium or laser show ticket or $3 without a show ticket. Check the Web site for complete schedule as well as laser show schedule.

■ ■ ■ ■ CLAMS AND CHAOS

The Shack (1 Stony Hollow Road/Route 25A, Centerport; 631-754-8989, www.clamsandchaos.com). This quintessential roadside fried fish stand is indeed dubbed "clams and chaos"—although the "chaos" is due to the treacherous parking along a busy stretch of 25A (mostly on evenings and weekends) rather than to the controlled activity taking place in the kitchen and behind the counter.

I've never seen Long Islanders on such good behavior: patiently waiting in line for their orders, taking turns at the dozen or so picnic tables—it's a soft-spoken, almost austere culinary atmosphere. Why? The food and fun atmosphere are that good.

The menu selections tally in at about $15 or less. Opt for a generously sized soft-shell crab sandwich that takes two hands to tackle. Complete the meal with sweet potato French fries, vinegar-based German-style slaw, and wash it all down with a Lighthouse Ale. A visit to the Shack is one of Long Island's finer moments. Open Apr. through Oct.

▪▪▪▪ NORTHPORT MAIN STREET (AND MORE) TOUR

Maroni Cuisine (18 Woodbine Avenue, Northport; 631-757-4500; www.maronicuisine.com). In a word: meatballs. But what a word it is. How good are Mike Maroni's meatballs? So good that "Grandma Maroni's Meatballs" (from where the recipe came) are a registered trademark. So good that the restaurant sells some 600 Maroni-style hot pots to go—a crisp white stove pot full of Maroni's homemade moist meatballs and pomodoro sauce ($22 for the personal size of eight meatballs and pasta—you get to keep the pot). So good that acclaimed chef Bobby Flay challenged Maroni to a Meatball Throwdown. Maroni won. But don't think this cozy gastronomic gem of only 32 seats is strictly Italian. It's not. Equally as popular as the meatballs is the 16-or-

so-course nightly tasting menu. The self-taught Maroni ditched his brick oven and pizza menu a few years back and now creates the cuisine he wants—you just happen to be there for the culinary ride of your life. The untraditional crowd-pleasing smorgasbord includes million-dollar potato chips (they're topped with caviar), octopus fra diavolo, and, of course, the Italian trio of eggplant parmigiana and those infamous meatballs with rigatoni pomodoro. The tasting menu changes weekly (the chalkboard comes with a question mark). This unique foodie adventure tallies in at a hefty $110 ($115–125 Fri. and Sat. seatings), wine included. Open Tues. to Sat. for lunch and dinner. Cash only. Same-day-only reservations a must.

Copenhagen Bakery (75 Woodbine Avenue, Northport; 631-754-3256). The place in town for tasty treats, rustic breads, sandwiches, and coffee. Eat your to-go treats across the street at the Northport Dock.

The Ritz Café (44 Woodbine Avenue, Northport; 631-754-6348; www.ritzcafenorthport.com). Nice space, inviting bar. Nightly entrées include pasta dishes (about $15–21) and fresh seafood, chicken, and steak plates (about $18–$34). Popular Sun. brunch as well ($12).

Tim's Shipwreck Diner (46 Main Street, Northport; 631-754-1797). Good affordable diner fare housed in a cozy vintage dining car setting. Lots of fun photos adorn the walls.

The Northport Sweet Shop (55 Main Street, 631-261-3748). How sweet it is. This family-owned luncheonette (a Northport staple for some 80 years) offers a simple menu where summer sandwiches feature homegrown organic tomatoes. But really go there for the homemade ice cream in traditional flavors such as rum raisin, black raspberry, and coconut.

Northport Tasting Room and Wine Cellar (70 Main Street, Northport; 631-261-0642; www.northportwines.com). A classy change of pace that's part wineshop, part tasting room. Live jazz and piano music, usually on Fri. and Sat.

Northport Feed & Grain (73 Main Street, Northport; 631-651-2685). The name of this popular casual eatery suggests more turf such as a variety of house burgers, but there's also plenty of surf, particularly the lobster roll served with corn on the cob and potato salad ($19). Nice outdoor terrace.

Harbor Trading (79 Main Street, Northport; 631-754-1653, www.northportcandy.com). Rows of colorful and tasty old-fashioned candy and sweet treats as far as the eye can see.

Cow Harbor Fine Gifts and Collectibles (101 Main Street, Northport; 631-261-6001). A Northport gift store essential for 15 years. For delicate home scents, whimsical nautical pottery, durable garden accessories, and quaint lighthouse collectibles.

TAS Design and Craft Gallery (106 Main Street, Northport; 631-539-6041). For unique colorful pottery, wind chimes, and beautiful delicate glass witch balls that will keep the bad spirits away.

The Dishmonger (146 Main Street, Northport; 631-239-1480). Elbows off the table! Tucked behind the tarot card reader storefront, Dishmonger offers a small but fine collection of tableware, cookware, fine linens, and oilcloths.

▮▮▮▮ OUTSIDE

Sunken Meadow State Park (Route 25A and Sunken Meadow Parkway, Kings Park; 631-269-4333 or 631-269-5351 for golf info; www.nysparks.state.ny.us). Officially known as Governor Alfred E. Smith/Sunken Meadow State Park (although everyone just calls it Sunken Meadow), this North Shore seaside retreat offers a ¾-

mile-long boardwalk and spectacular views of the Long Island Sound. In addition you'll find a golf course, driving range, and a popular but challenging cross-country running course.

Fees cost $8 or use your Empire Passport.

Nissequogue River State Park (799 Saint Johnland Road, Kings Park; 631-269-4927; www.nys parks.state.ny.us). Most folks look toward Long Island's north and south shores to find tranquil calm in the form of a waterside sanctuary (most notably the Long Island Sound and the Atlantic Ocean), but Long Island has a few rivers to call its own. The Nissequogue is one of them. A newcomer to the state park system, Nissequogue River State Park joined the ranks in 1999. A portion of its grounds include acreage and abandoned buildings from the now-defunct Kings Park Psychiatric Center. The space offers hiking, a nature trail, and boat rentals available through Nissequogue River Canoe & Kayak Rentals at 631-979-8244.

∎∎∎∎ WATERFRONT

Northport Village Dock (Woodbine Avenue and Main Street, Northport) provides ample parking for your Main Street stroll as well as picturesque views of Northport Harbor.

Betty Allen Twin Ponds Nature Park (Route 25A/Fort Salonga Road, Centerport). Named after a local community activist, this 30-acre preserve offers nature trails and some North Shore solitude. Open year-round. Free admission.

∎∎∎∎ PERFORMANCE

John W. Engeman Theater (250 Main Street, Northport; 631-261-2900; johnwengemantheater .com). This small community theater is big on Broadway-style plays, musicals, and children's performances. Northport's theater history began in 1912 with a movie and vaudeville house next door (the original burned down in 1932). A new movie house was built in the 1950s, but the eventual rise of the multiplex a few decades later saw the Northport Theater reduced to second-run and discount film status. It was transformed into a live performance theater venue, purchased by Patti and Kevin O'Neill in 2006, and renamed in honor of Patti's brother, who died in service in Iraq in 2006. Tickets start at about $50. Stick around for drinks afterward at the on-site Green Room Piano Bar and Lounge.

∎∎∎∎ SHOP

The Vanderbilt Museum Gift Shop in the planetarium is out of this world. For astronomy- and natural history–themed gifts. Call 631-854-5534.

■ ■ ■ ■ SPECIAL EVENTS

Monthly: **Night sky observatory sessions** hosted by the Astronomical Society of Long Island at the Vanderbilt Planetarium.

Summer: **Long Island Sound Saunter.** Held in late August, this two-hour summer stroll tours where the Nissequogue River meets the Long Island Sound. About $4 for adults. Registration required at 631-581-1072

September: **Cow Harbor Day** celebrates all things Northport, which was once known as Great Cow Harbor.

Late October: **Vanderbilt Car Show** at the Vanderbilt Museum.

■ ■ ■ ■ STAY

Chalet Inn & Suites (23 Centershore Road, Centerport; 631-757-4600; www.chaletinnandsuites.com). Better than basic accommodations not far from the Vanderbilt mansion.

■ ■ ■ ■ LIRR OPTION/ LOCAL TAXI INFO

The Vanderbilt Museum is about a 3-mile cab ride from either the Greenlawn or Northport train stations (Port Jefferson branch). Orange and White Taxi in East Northport (631-261-0235) pro-

vides service from the Northport station for about $13 for one person; about $16 for two people.

■ ■ ■ ■ READS AND RESOURCES

Visit the **Village of Northport** at www.villageofnorthport.com.

Visit the **Nissequogue River Foundation** at www.ourstatepark .com.

Read *The Long Island Motor Parkway* by Howard Kroplick and Al Velocci.

■ ■ ■ ■ NEXT STOP

In keeping with the natural history theme of the Vanderbilt visit, nearby Smithtown offers a unique slice of Suffolk's North Shore in the great outdoors.

Sweetbriar Nature Center (62 Eckernkamp Drive, Smithtown; 631-979-6344; www.sweetbriarnc .org). A not-for-profit 54-acre wildlife and nature center for kids of all ages. Sweetbriar hosts seasonal outdoor activities for schoolkids—such as a butterfly house and summer camp—and also hosts a photography club and artists' workshops for adults.

Smithtown Historical Society (239 Middle Country Road, Smithtown; 631-265-6768; www .smithtownhistorical.org). All those Smiths—it really is Smithtown after all. The Smithtown Historical Society oversees some

14 historical properties, including the Caleb Smith House, the Judge J. Lawrence Smith House, and the Epenetus Smith Tavern. Most houses are located on the main site; other structures make for a historical heritage treasure hunt in the surrounding neighborhoods. The historical society provides info and maps on them all.

Caleb Smith State Park Preserve (581 West Jericho Turnpike, Smithtown; 631-265-1054; www.nysparks.state.ny.us). Includes some 500-plus acres of beautifully unspoiled Long Island natural habitats including freshwater wetlands, ponds, streams, fields, and woodland. Activities include hiking, fishing, cross-country skiing, and a small nature museum that hosts family-themed science walks. Open Wed. through Sun.

MAIN STREETS
AND A SHOPPING MALL

6 • DINNER AND AN ART HOUSE MOVIE IN HUNTINGTON: *Cinema Arts Centre*

Huntington, Cold Spring Harbor, Lloyd Harbor

Bye-bye, summer Hollywood blockbuster.

Move over, mainstream multiplex.

Sorry, DreamWorks and Disney—you don't stand a chance.

At Cinema Arts Centre in Huntington, *indy* isn't slang for a city, and a subtitle is a very stupendous thing.

Cinema Arts Centre, CAC, has been bursting the Hollywood bubble with a world of independent, foreign, and art house films since 1973. It has also been a labor of love for codirector and cofounder Vic Skolnick.

"We were escapees from the city," Skolnick said. He started CAC with his lifelong partner Charlotte Sky.

"We were avid, more than avid filmgoers," he said. "We were deep into film."

Skolnick, who grew up in Brooklyn, says that New York City during the 1950s and 1960s enjoyed a tremendous variety of independent theaters.

"We always ventured to Manhattan for a movie," he said. "It was my graduate school."

Soon Skolnick and Sky moved to Manhattan, and, ultimately, to the suburbs of Long Island. Once on Long Island, the ever-engaging octogenarian says the only thing available "was single-screen Hollywood stuff." He and Sky, self-proclaimed exiles from New York City, would travel to the city with son Dylan in tow just to see a movie.

"My son grew up in the cinema," Skolnick said. "Parents who are theater people say their children grew up in a trunk. We say Dylan grew up in a film can." Dylan Skolnick is now codirector of CAC.

After traveling back and forth to Manhattan just to see a movie, Skolnick and Sky thought they can't be the only two suburban transplants who occasionally wanted to watch a foreign film.

"Sixty miles just to catch a movie? So we acted on that assumption that there was a need for people who wanted a different kind of venue. That was the push."

The rest is its own version of cinematic history.

"So in 1973, we started the cinema as an escape, in a sense, or a return to a program that we used to enjoy," Skolnick said. "And now we had the option of creating it ourselves. Pretty much that's what we've done for the past 36 or so years."

Skolnick says CAC first screened films using a Bell & Howell 16mm library projector.

"We started with nothing," he said. "It was a slow, gradual build."

Although the CAC has always been in Huntington, previous locations included a dance studio and a former Huntington firehouse. The current CAC home began as the auditorium of an elementary school.

"Since then we've transformed the place," Skolnick said.

Folks call CAC a movie art house, but "we call ourselves an independent community cinema."

Skolnick explains that the world of showing movies comes in tiers: commercial first-runs and second-tier smaller independent stock. And that's why you'll never see a mainstream Hollywood movie at CAC. He adds that CAC has a simple rule.

"We watch everything we put on our program."

Skolnick and Sky screen one or two films a night—an easier task during the last few decades with the arrival of video and DVD. How many films has he seen in his lifetime? He ponders the question with a quick calculation: at least eight a week, multiplied by 52 weeks a year, multiplied by decades.

"Thousands," Skolnick replies. "And Charlotte insists on watching films to the end. So it could have been more. I have a short fuse."

He'll pass on a film if he doesn't like it.

"I say 'next,' and she'll say, 'I'm watching it.'"

Over the years one viewing screen at CAC led to two. Two screens led to three. Today CAC sells some 200,000 tickets a year.

"That's one person coming a lot," Skolnick quips.

In addition, CAC boasts some 8,000 members. It was one of those members who, back in 1988, donated $1 million to CAC.

"That donation transformed the cinema from a beat-up old auditorium to a pretty nice-looking joint," Skolnick said.

CAC now includes a small café and a 2,500-square-foot community space. Special events host guest filmmakers, concerts, and readings.

"People like to stay a while after a movie and talk," Skolnick said. "It became a schmooze."

The biggest blockbuster CAC has ever screened was Roberto Begnini's *Life Is Beautiful*. "People saw it who said they'd never see a subtitled film." The film began its run during midsummer and continued through the following year. *Life Is Beautiful* enjoyed commercial success as well.

Skolnick reiterates the grand world of film that lives outside the mainstream Hollywood bubble: "That's our premise. We're a film window on the world."

▄▄▄▄ INFO

Cinema Arts Centre is open daily. Tickets cost $9 at all times. Discounts are given to members, students, seniors, and children. Call 631-423-7611 or visit www .cinemaartscentre.org.

▄▄▄▄ GETTING THERE

Cinema Arts Centre is at 423 Park Avenue in Huntington, just south of Route 25A/Main Street. Take the L.I.E. exit 49N or the Northern State Parkways exit 40N, which is Route 110. Continue north along Route 110 through Huntington Station, past the train station, and into Huntington Village. Turn right on Main Street/Route 25A. Go three traffic lights to Park Avenue and turn right.

▄▄▄▄ EAT HUNTINGTON VILLAGE TOUR

Huntington Village on a Friday or Saturday night buzzes with activity. The vibe is very lighthearted and the age range runs the gamut. There are dozens of restaurants from which to choose that offer a little something for everyone. This isn't a complete list but a good place to start.

American Roadside Burgers (337 New York Avenue, Huntington; 631-935-0300; www.roadside burgers.com). Thrifty good burgers in a fun rustic setting. Devouring a Roadstar—four cheeseburgers on one bun ($7.61)—gets your name on the Roadside Wall of Fame. Open daily for lunch and dinner.

Skorpios (340 New York Avenue, Huntington; 631-549-8887; www.skorpioslongisland .com). Of the two informal restos that offer authentic Greek specialties in Huntington Village (they stand practically side by side), Skorpios gets the edge. Why? It's Greek to me. Open daily for lunch and dinner. Entrées cost $9–21.

Honu Kitchen and Cocktails (363 New York Avenue, Huntington; 631-421-6900; www.honu kitchen.com). Honu bustles with the North Shore's young and beautiful. These trendy digs offer contemporary American fare, moderate portions, and reasonable prices. Open for dinner Tues. through Sun. Mains $8–21.

Red Bar & Restaurant (417 New York Avenue, Huntington; 631-673-0304; www.redrestaurantli.com). For quality food, light ambiance, and pleasant decor, Red is as reliable as they come. For satisfying steaks, fresh fish dishes, and Italian-style rustic fare. The three-course Sun. to Thurs. prix fixe menu ($32) is a pretty good deal. Open weekdays for lunch; daily for dinner.

Samurai Japanese Steakhouse (46A Gerard Street; 631-271-2588; www.samuraihibachi.com). Samurai provides Japanese beef and seafood fare with a grill-side seat complete with slicing, dicing, and culinary wizardry as chefs prepare your meal at an open-style hibachi. Sushi and bento boxes as well. The loyal local following means reservations are required. Open Tues. through Sun. late afternoons for dinner. Hibachi entrées $14–35.

Café Buenos Aires (23 Wall Street, Huntington; 631-603-3600; www.cafebuenosaires.net). Tango with your tapas? Yes, you can, during Sunday brunch at Café Buenos Aires, a popular Argentinean-style eatery that offers dozens of hot and cold tapas selections, such as black angus, portobello, and Brie cheese solomillo; mixed grill and brochettes; and a generous selection of Argentinean wines. Open daily for lunch and dinner. Tapas costs $5–12.

Crumbs Bake Shop (11 Wall Street, Huntington; 631-421-4500; www.crumbs.com). This Huntington location is one of a chain of two dozen-plus dessert shops that started in New York City in 2003. Their fresh signature desserts can be summed up in three words: red velvet cupcakes. That's all you need to know. Open 'til midnight on Fri. and Sat.

Bistro Cassis (55B Wall Street, Huntington; 631-421-4122; www.bistrocassis.com). French food and flair deserves a nod in Huntington Village. Cassis most definitely gets the job done with authentic lovely decor, good prices, and fresh ingredients. Open daily for lunch and dinner. Popular Sunday brunch. Entrées $19–29.

Quetzalcoatl (296 Main Street, Huntington; 631-427-7834; www.quetzalcoatlmexrest.com). It's pronounced ketz-a-co-tel. The newer Mexican restaurant in Huntington Village gets points for ambiance, friendly service, and solid Mexican specialties. Open daily for lunch and dinner; Sun. for breakfast/brunch as well. Entrées cost $11–34.

Munday's (259 Main Street,

*Book Revue,
Huntington*

Huntington; 631-421-3553). Very good diner and luncheonette fare with generous portions and decent prices any day of the week. Open from morning 'til night and Sun. for breakfast and lunch.

Ariana Restaurant Café (255 Main Street, Huntington; 631-421-2933; www.arianacafe.com). Adjacent to Munday's, Ariana offers exotic Middle Eastern flavors. The Afghan specialty starters include luscious Aushak Kadu—homemade ravioli filled with roasted pumpkin topped with meat sauce and mint yogurt dressing ($8). Dinner entrées (about $20–27) include tender well-cooked lamb dishes and great vegetarian options as well. Open daily for lunch and dinner; Sun. for dinner.

▮▮▮▮ SHOP

Heli Sport (308 New York Avenue, Huntington; 631-549-1127). Sports fans to the front of the line. Quality sporting goods supply for all-season sports enthusiasts.

Book Revue (313 New York Avenue, Huntington; 631-271-1442; www.bookrevue.com). The indy bookstore lives! Not as polished as their mall or big box counterparts, the family-owned unpretentious but serious Book Revue has been a Huntington staple since 1977. It offers two floors of new and used titles and a young and very friendly staff. It also attracts some pretty big names for book signings. Past guests have included Ray Bradbury, Frank McCourt, Joyce Carol Oates, Garrison Keillor, and David Sedaris, and more recently Paula Deen, Joan Rivers, and Nicolas Sparks. For book lovers, it doesn't get better than this. Open daily; Fri. and Sat. nights until 11 PM.

Just Kids Nostalgia (342 New York Avenue, Huntington; 631-423-8449; www.justkidsnostalgia

.com). Pop culture kitsch and collectibles for kids of all ages. Just Kids offers vintage movie posters, collectible comic books, vinyl records, and the occasional impromptu live performance in the storefront window.

Greentique (334 New York Avenue, Huntington; 631-427-2090; www.greentiqueonline .com). Go green! Take an old canvas sail or even a discarded chocolate chip cookie package and give it new life by recycling it into the likes of a fun and colorful tote bag or clutch.

Ben's Garden (344 New York Avenue, Huntington; 631-427-3250; www.bensgarden.com). For one-a-kind garden-themed gifts and ornaments, unique paperweights, and original découpage. Also in Oyster Bay (95 Audrey Avenue; 516-922-7646).

b.j. spoke gallery (299 Main Street, Huntington; 516-549-5106; www.bjspokegallery.com). How artsy is it? The lowercase name says it all. A fine and contemporary art gallery cooperative in the heart of Huntington for some two decades. Closed Mon.

Cow Over the Moon Sports Art (302 Main Street, Huntington; 631-424-1796; www.cowoverthe moonsportsart.com). The place is packed to the rafters. For unique gifts and sports-themed items such as autographed framed photographs of your favorite sports stars to unique custom-made sports art personalized with a loved one's favorite sport, their name, and jersey number.

Walt Whitman Mall (at the intersection of Route 110 and Jericho Turnpike, Huntington Station; 631-271-1741; www.walt whitmanmall.com). If you've the need for a dose of mall-style shopping, Walt Whitman is about 4 miles south of Huntington Village. Anchor stores include Macy's, Lord & Taylor, Bloomingdale's, and Saks Fifth Avenue. Signature stores include Abercrombie & Fitch, Banana Republic, Coach, and Brooks Brothers. There are about 100 stores in all. Restaurants include Legal Sea Foods and the Cheesecake Factory.

▮▮▮▮ OUTSIDE

Caumsett State Historic Park (25 Lloyd Harbor Road, Huntington; 631-423-1770; www.nysparks .state.ny.us). This tranquil space just north of Huntington Village provides hiking, biking, fishing, bridle paths, and cross-country skiing. The Marshall Field estate built in 1921 remains on-site. Open year-round from sunrise to 5 PM weekdays and to 8 PM weekends. Admission costs $8 per vehicle Apr. through Nov. or use your Empire Passport.

■■■■ SIGHTSEE

Heckscher Museum of Art (2 Prime Avenue located along Route 25A, one traffic light east of the Route 110 intersection, Huntington; 631-351-3250; www .heckscher.org). A small but wonderful resource for museum-generated art exhibitions in town. Open Tues. through Fri. and weekend afternoons. Admission costs about $6 for adults; $4 for students and seniors.

Walt Whitman Birthplace (246 Old Walt Whitman Road, West Hills; 631-427-5247; www.walt whitman.org). The official title is Walt Whitman Birthplace State Historic Site and Interpretive Center. The small farmhouse, administered by the Walt Whitman Birthplace Association, dates to 1810 and is indeed the birthplace of one of America's most-loved poets. The house was built by Whitman's father. Whitman was born in 1819. The space offers a

Visitors Center and guided tours, hosts a poet-in-residence, and awards the Long Island Poet of the Year. Open daily mid-June through Labor Day; during summer; Wed. through Sun. in winter. $5 for adults.

■■■■ SPECIAL EVENTS

Summer: **Huntington Summer Arts Festival**. A concert series held outdoors at Heckscher Park. Visit www.huntingtonarts.org.

Early September: Annual *Song of Myself* **Marathon** at the Walt Whitman Birthplace.

■■■■ STAY

Oheka Castle Hotel & Estate (135 West Gate Drive, Huntington; 631-659-1400; www.oheka.com). This superb Gold Coast treasure was built by financier and philanthropist Otto Kahn between 1914 and 1919. Kahn built the French-style chateau on the highest point on Long Island. After

Heckscher Museum

■■■■ **LONG ISLAND RESTAURANT WEEK**

It's all in good taste!

In the first week of November, some 50 Island-wide restaurants offer a special three-course prix fixe menu for about $25. It's a great way to sample the culinary ingenuity of many fine local restaurants without breaking the bank. Visit www.longislandrestaurantweek.com.

Huntington Village loves its food—and foodies—so much that they host their own version in mid-Oct.

changing hands and being abandoned and vandalized, Oheka Castle was purchased and painstakingly renovated in the 1980s. With its well-manicured grounds and sumptuous architecture, today Oheka Castle hosts weddings and special occasions and provides day visits and overnight stays. It also enjoys status on the National Register of Historic Places. Room rates start at $395 a night. Guided mansion tours cost $25 for adults. The address is listed as Huntington, but it's a half mile from the Cold Spring Harbor LIRR station.

■■■■ **LIRR OPTION/ LOCAL TAXI INFO**

Huntington Village is 2 miles north of the Huntington LIRR station (Huntington branch) at New York Avenue/Route 110 and Broadway. Crown Taxi (631-427-1166) provides cab service to CAC—$8 for the one-way fare.

■■■■ **FYI**

At 109,000 square feet and 127 rooms, Oheka Castle mentioned above is considered the second-largest private residence ever built in the United States. And this was Kahn's summer home!

A word of note: Heckscher Park in Huntington is a small park home to the Heckscher Museum of Art. Heckscher State Park is a New York State—run park located on the Great South Bay in East Islip (see Chapter 15).

■■■■ **READS AND RESOURCES**

Leaves of Grass is one of Walt Whitman's better-known works.

Visit the **Huntington Chamber of Commerce** at www.huntington chamber.com.

■■■■ **NEXT STOP**

If driving into Huntington along Route 25A from points west, you'll no doubt pass through the small but scenic stretch of Cold Spring Harbor. Two stops are well known.

Cold Spring Harbor Hatchery and Aquarium (1660 Route 25A/Route 108 on the border of Nassau and Suffolk, Cold Spring Harbor; 516-692-6768; www.csh fha.org).

The family that fishes together . . . eats fish for dinner together. A popular stop for families, the Cold Spring Harbor Hatchery has been a freshwater fish hatchery for more than a century—it celebrated its 125th anniversary in 2008. In recent decades it has become an education facility on local fish, amphibians, and reptiles. The space features two aquarium buildings, eight outdoor ponds, and Tiny, the resident 79-pound snapping turtle. And yes, you can fish, but you need to keep what you catch (remember, catch all that you want, but eat all that you catch!).

Fishing is available first come, first served Fri. through Tues. late mornings, and early afternoons in June, July, and Aug. Open daily. Admission costs about $6 for adults; $4 for students and seniors. The fishing session costs an extra $5. All trout caught costs $4 per fish. You can bring your own fishing equipment or rent a rod and reel on-site.

Cold Spring Harbor Whaling Museum (Main Street, Cold Spring Harbor; 631-367-3418; www.cshwhalingmuseum.org). Welcome landlubbers. An institution in these parts since 1942, the museum chronicles Cold Spring Harbor's and Long Island's once bustling whaling industry with exhibitions, permanent displays, and children's programs. Open daily. About $6 for adults; $5 for students and seniors. The adjacent Main Street stretch offers a quick stroll of specialty shops, cafés, and parking.

7 • CURTAIN CALLS IN PORT JEFFERSON: *Theatre Three*

Port Jefferson, Port Jefferson Station, Stony Brook, St. James

Broadway meets Main Street at Theatre Three.

The epitome of vibrant community theater, Theatre Three offers an intimate live theater experience and garners tons of local support. This may very well be the highlight of your Port Jeff visit.

Executive artistic director Jeffrey Sanzel says Theatre Three was founded in 1969 by three local theater professionals who lived in the Three Village area. They moved into the building in 1979.

"It was created in the little theater movement of the late '60s, early '70s," said Sanzel. "It started with more cutting edge theater. They would do the Greeks, Pirandello. And as it grew it became both an artistic venue and a commercial theater."

Sanzel says local community theater based on Long Island does have a few challenges.

"Mainly that we're so close to the theater capitol of the world in New York City," he said. "People do have that option."

Being in Broadway's shadow means that small independent

local theaters such as Theatre Three can't duplicate a production if the show is currently running on the Great White Way.

"So we try to offer the intimacy of a 400-seat theater instead of, say, a 1,500-seat space."

The Theatre Three season, which runs from July through the following June, consists of four musicals, two plays, and the ever popular annual production of *A Christmas Carol*.

"That in itself is a Long Island family tradition," Sanzel said. The holiday classic has been an annual staple at Theatre Three since the mid-1980s.

Other recent productions included big-name Broadway musicals and dramas such as *The Wedding Singer, Smoky Joe's Café, The Producers, The Graduate,* and *Little Shop of Horrors*. Theatre Three also hosts cabaret and comedy events, a children's theater, theater workshops and classes, and an annual festival of one-act plays.

"For the one-act-play festival, we receive about 700 submissions from around the world," Sanzel said. Of that number, a lucky six enjoy their world premieres at Theatre Three.

In addition, the space is simply a stunner, too—productions are held at Athena Hall, a 125-year-old historic building.

"Our goal has always been for variety," Sanzel said. "There's something for everyone here at some time in the year."

■■■■ INFO

Single admission seats are a bargain and start at $14. Yearly subscription packages let you purchase seven shows for about the price of five. Call the box office at 631-928-9100 or visit www.theatre three.com.

■■■■ GETTING THERE

Theatre Three is at 412 Main Street in Port Jefferson. Access Main Street as well as the Port Jeffer-

son/Bridgeport Ferry by taking the L.I.E. to exit 64. Continue north on Route 112 to Port Jefferson Village.

■■■■ PORT JEFFERSON/ BRIDGEPORT FERRY

Say Port Jefferson and one of the first things that come to mind is the ferry. The Bridgeport and Port Jefferson Steamboat Company offers up to 11 departures daily (weekends). The trip takes about one hour and 15 minutes. A one-way fare (car and driver) costs about $51. Other fees apply for additional passengers and motorcycles. Call 631-473-0286 or visit www.bpjferry.com.

The New England Tours division of the ferry offers a variety of year-round tours if you wish to escape Long Island for a day or two and begin the adventure with a mini boat cruise. Tour themes highlight New England ski

Port Jefferson Ferry

resorts, casinos, the Mystic Seaport and Aquarium, Newport mansions, and Boston, to name a few. Visit the complete list of tours online or contact 631-473-5138. To access the ferry, follow the directions above, then turn right on East Main Street, left on East Broadway, and a right into the ferry lot.

■ ■ ■ ■ WATERFRONT

Harborfront Park and **Harborfront Park Community Center** (Port Jefferson Village Center, East Broadway; 631-802-2160 for the Community Center www.portjeff.com/harborfront and www.pjvillagecenter.com). Adjacent to the ferry dock and Danford's Inn, Harborfront Park is a tranquil spot to watch the ferry depart and arrive. The 5-acre waterfront property includes a promenade, pier, picnic area, and playground. Also nearby is the Chandlery building, a former maritime supply store that dates to 1898. The open, airy Community Center hosts special events, art exhibitions, the Children's Maritime Museum, and an outdoor skating rink during winter.

■ ■ ■ ■ EAT PORT JEFFERSON

The Catch (111 West Broadway, Port Jefferson; 631-642-2824; www.thecatchtavern.com). One of the better options for seafood in Port Jeff. This seafood tavern offers good fare, outdoor terrace seating, and picturesque harbor views. The all-you-can-eat popular Sunday brunch costs about $29.50, but that includes lobster and crab. Clambake Mondays feature lobster, mussels, steamers, and vegetable for about $16 from 4 PM—closing. Open daily.

Fifth Season (34 East Broadway, Port Jefferson; 631-477-8500; www.thefifth-season.com). You will be inspired by Fifth Season because Fifth Season is inspired by the likes of fresh seafood, organic Long Island ingredients, and inventive American cuisine. The $28 Sun. through Thurs. prix fixe dinner is a bargain. Sample organic chicken wontons with pineapple-coconut dip for starters; grilled ahi tuna with roasted vegetable ratatouille, and top it all off with a seasonal berry sponge cake. Open weekdays for lunch, weekends for brunch, and daily for dinner.

The Village Way (106 Main Street, Port Jefferson; 631-928-3395; www.villagewayrestaurant.com). This is another popular resto that's insanely busy when the village is hoppin'—that's because there's a little something for everyone, particularly families, at fair to moderate prices. Inventive menu, too, including a children's menu, Sunday brunch, early bird special, pasta night ($14.95 on Thurs. 3 PM—closing), and a unique seasonal Old English Dickens prix fixe ($29.95) menu that includes English Yorkshire pudding, Christmas goose, and bread pudding dessert. Online coupons, too. Open daily.

Long Island's Best Desserts (104 Main Street, Port Jefferson; 631-403-4616). Do they live up to their name? They're pretty darn close. A sweet way to end your Port Jeff visit. The place gets crazy busy when there's a crowd in town. That means tables are at a premium, especially on the outdoor deck. But you're ordering *chocolate cake*, so be patient and just go with the flow.

Salsa Salsa (142 Main Street, Port Jefferson; 631-473-9700; www.salsasalsa.net). Its official name is Salsa Salsa A Burrito Bar but you can get much more than that. A seriously delicious Mexican restaurant.

Toast Coffeehouse (242 East Main Street, Port Jefferson; 631-331-6860; www.toastcoffeehouse .com). Perhaps the coziest vibe in town. Probably because it's just off the beaten path—a relaxed break from a busy summer night scene on the Main Street strip. For breakfast (the Down Port omelet includes crab, asparagus, bacon, roasted red pepper, and smoked

Gouda, $12), lunch, fondue ($25 per couple), tapas (shrimp and cashew wontons, $10), cheese plates, and wine.

Colosseo Pizza and Restaurant (1049 Route 112, Port Jefferson Station; 631-928-4972). It's not exactly on the Main Street strip, but if you're en route to catch the ferry, first catch a serious slice— or two—to go.

■ ■ ■ ■ SHOP

Boardwalk Games (98 Main Street, Port Jefferson; 631-928-4263; www.shop.boardwalk gamesinc.com). Boardwalk Games does justice to its prime corner location, creating busy in-store traffic and buzz while paying proper homage to a time-honored recession-proof form of family entertainment: the board game. The well-stocked inventory includes Monopoly in fun collectible versions such as the New York Mets, *Seinfeld*, the Beatles, and a first edition all in wood—a popular seller. The special chess sets include an American League MLB showdown with versions in the New York Yankees and the Boston Red Sox. Very fun to browse. Friendly, helpful staff. Open daily high season.

Not Too Shabby (12 Chandler Square, Port Jefferson: 631-828-4269). Fun-to-browse for second-hand gently used clothes, jewelry, and vintage housewares that look, well, not too...

Castaways (25 Chandler Square, Port Jefferson; 631-473-6333; www.saveapetli.net). The retail store of the local Save-A-Pet Animal Rescue and Adoption Center. Doggie treats, animal supplies, and gifts.

The East End Shirt Co. (3 Mill Creek Road, Port Jefferson; 631-473-2093; www.eastendco.com). For retail and wholesale silkscreen products. The store stocks colorful, not overly done Port Jeff— and nautical-themed T-shirts and some just plain funny ones, too: "It's fun until someone loses an eye" states one T-shirt. The visual shows four bandanna-clad pirates, the last one wearing a black eye-patch over one eye. Arrrrrrrrrrrrrrrrr! Very friendly and helpful staff.

Harbor Square Mall (134 Main Street, Port Jefferson). The tired layout and look is reminiscent of a retail remnant of bygone era. It could use a little sprucing up, but that just adds to the charm. Vendors include Pepperheads Hot Sauces, Your Favorite Team sports paraphernalia, and Sea Creations nautical-themed gifts and seashells (631-473-8388).

Village Chairs and Wares (120 East Main Street, Port Jefferson; 631-331-5791; www.villagechairs andwares.com). Rustic tables and chairs, exterior wood shutters, and farmhouse Shaker reproductions.

Pattern Finders (128 East Main Street, Port Jefferson; 631-928-5158). Pattern Finders and neighboring Etcetera Consignment Boutique offer packed-to-the-rafters-style china patterns, antiques, and treasures.

Port Jefferson Free Library (150 East Main Street, Port Jefferson; 631-473-0022; www.portjeff library.org). Offers a Friends of the Library used book shop (open during the day) in a quaint maritime setting along the original Main Street. The retail building dates to 1848, says their Web site. History buffs should take an online peek at the well-researched history of the library, which comes complete with wonderful vintage photos.

▆▆▆▆ SIGHTSEE

Mather House Museum and Spinney Clock Exhibit Museum (115 Prospect Street, Port Jefferson; 631-473-2665; www.portjeff historical.org). What time is it? Time to visit the 1840s-era Mather House complex, five historical buildings run by the Historical Society of Greater Port Jefferson. The Mather House is home to ship artifacts, maritime memorabilia, and period furnishings, and the Spinney Clock Exhibit Museum boasts an impressive collection of some 250 clocks. Open July and Aug. afternoons Tues., Wed., Sat., and Sun.

■ ■ ■ ■ SPECIAL EVENTS

Summer: **Music in the Park** free outdoor concert series in Port Jefferson Village.

July: **Stony Brook Film Festival** (www.stonybrookfilmfestival .com).

Early December: **Port Jefferson Dickens Festival.** Spreading holiday cheer complete with fancy Victorian costumes since 1996. Held at various locations in Port Jeff Village. Visit the Greater Port Jefferson Arts Council at www.gpj ac.org/dickens.

■ ■ ■ ■ STAY

Danford's Hotel and Marina (25 East Broadway, Port Jefferson; 866-309-0508 www.danfords .com). Port Jeff wouldn't be Port Jeff without the ferry, Theatre Three, and, of course, Danford's. The sprawling hotel complex located directly on the harbor-front boasts 86 rooms and suites decorated in tasteful nautical flair; a 75-slip marina; a fitness center and spa; a conference center; and plenty of places to eat including a waterfront restaurant, a trendy lounge, and an al fresco dining option as well. Room rates about $249–549 per night.

Ransome Inn B&B (409 E. Broadway, Port Jefferson, 631-474-5019; www.ransomeinn.net). If you prefer something a bit off the bustle of Main Street, Ransome Inn offers intimate rooms inspired by a country visit in a Cape Cod–style home that dates to 1868. There's also a 900-square-foot carriage house for rent (over the two-car garage) about $200 for the weekend.

■ ■ ■ ■ DRIVING TIPS

Parking comes at a premium on busy summer nights, especially Fridays and Saturdays. The key is to just pick an aisle in the public pay parking lot (behind the strip of Main Street stores) and patiently wait with your flashers on until someone leaves.

■ ■ ■ ■ LIRR OPTIONS/ LOCAL TAXI INFO

Port Jefferson Village is accessible from the Port Jefferson station (Port Jefferson branch). The LIRR offers a package deal for about $25 that includes discounted round-trip rail fare to and from Manhattan, two Lindy's Taxi vouchers (631-851-0000), and discount coupons good at participating Port Jeff merchants and restaurants. LIRR also offers a Port Jeff Ferry discount as well.

■ ■ ■ ■ **FYI**

The Bridgeport and Port Jefferson Steamboat Company was founded in 1883. It currently accommodates some 440,000 vehicles and nearly one million passengers every year.

■ ■ ■ ■ **READS AND RESOURCES**

Visit the **Port Jefferson Chamber of Commerce** at www.portjeff chamber.com.

Visit **Discover Stony Brook Village Center** at www.stony brookvillage.com.

■ ■ ■ ■ **NEXT STOP**

With Port Jeff as your base, nearby St. James and Stony Brook provide historical museum and heritage visits, and a little night music, too.

St. James General Store (516 Moriches Road, St. James; 631-854-3740). The St. James General Store is considered the oldest general store in the country that's still open for business. It dates to 1857 and today offers the likes of vintage-style handcrafts, candies, and preserves.

Stony Brook Grist Mill (100 Harbor Road off Main Street, Stony Brook; 631-751-2244; www .wmho.org). Operated by the Ward Melville Heritage Organization, this working gristmill dates to the 1750s and is listed on the National Register of Historic Places. Open weekend afternoons early May through early Dec. About $2 for adults.

Long Island Museum of American Art, History, and Carriages (1200 Route 25A, Stony Brook; 631-751-0066; www.long islandmuseum.org). A wonderful and important resource that highlights Long Island's—and America's—cultural heritage. The museum boats an impressive collection of some 40,000 historical artifacts, objects, and artworks that date from the late 1700s as well as a lovely collection of 200 vintage carriages. Open Fri., Sat., and Sun. About $9 for adults.

Staller Center for the Arts (At SUNY Stony Brook, Stony Brook; 631-632-2787; www.stallercenter .com). The 1,050-seat Staller Center offers stellar live music, theater, and innovative dance performances Sept. through May.

8 • MAIN STREET STROLLS IN GREENPORT

Greenport, Orient, Shelter Island

For quaint Long Island charm, Greenport's got it all.

Whenever my Nassau County friends and I need a one-day escape, we always easily agree on Greenport. We know what to expect, but the trip always provides a dose of exactly what we need: a great meal, a Main Street stroll, a few kitschy museums and attractions, some beautiful waterside scenery, fun-to-browse art galleries and antiques shops, my favorite variety store in all the land, and friendly locals who simply love where they live.

Greenport may very well be your perfect day trip or unique Long Island weekend escape. You can take the train and stay overnight if you wish. You can also easily access the North Fork's vineyards and beaches. It's good for any hurried Long Island soul. Here is some of the best that Greenport has to offer.

▌▌▌▌ GETTING THERE

Take the L.I.E. to exit 73. Then take Route 25 east directly into Greenport.

▌▌▌▌ SIGHTSEE

East End Seaport Museum (631-477-2100; www.eastendseaport .org). A shore bet! The East End Maritime Museum packs in some magnificent maritime might in its small two-floor space complete with local fishing industry lore, model ships, and lighthouse lenses. Fun gift store, too. The $2 admission is an absolute bargain. The seasonal museum is open weekends Mid-May through June and Sept.; daily (except Tues.) July and Aug.

Greenport Carousel (Mitchell Park on Front Street). Will make your head spin! This glass-enclosed carousel dates to the 1920s and once stood at the Grumman picnic grounds in Calverton. It's been a centerpiece draw in Greenport since 1996. Catch the brass ring and get a free ride. Open daily during summer; weekends and holidays during low season.

▌▌▌▌ EAT GREENPORT

**Bruce's Cheese Emporium &
Café** (208 Main Street, Greenport;

631-477-0023). Can you live on bread (and cheese) alone? Yes. Tasty omelets and sandwiches to stay or go, too. Open daily July and Aug.; seasonal days and hours fall and winter.

Claudio's Restaurant (111 Main Street, Greenport; 631-477-0627; www.claudios.com). A serious seafood commodity in Greenport since 1870. You can't miss it—there's often a line of motorcycles parked in front. Claudio's Friday Night Bake includes a combo of Alaskan king crab legs, jumbo shrimp, clams, mussels, steamers, corn on the cob, and red potato. And what a catch it is—it costs $21 on Friday ($29 the rest of the week) and is served in a fun net bag. The restaurant also offers a generous Long Island North Fork wine list as well. Claudio's also operates the more casual Claudio's Clam Bar and Crabby Jerry's on the adjacent outdoor dock. Open daily for lunch, dinner, and Sunday brunch.

Frisky Oyster (27 Front Street, Greenport; 631-477-4265; www.thefriskyoyster.com) and **Frisky Oyster Bar** (106 Main Street, Greenport; 631-477-6720; www.friskybar.com). Two locations, same management, deliciously common theme: simple, simple, simple but inventive seafood menus (aren't those the best kind?). Entrées from $19—26.

BBQ Bill's Famous Texas Barbecue (47 Front Street, Greenport; 631-477-2300; www.bbqbills restaurant.com). For cold beer and really good BBQ. The combo two-meat sandwich (about $14) always satisfies—opt for the pulled pork and rather tasty sausage. Top the sandwich off with a heaping helping of creamy slaw. The service is always pleasant. And the kids can stare at the scale model train for hours. As for the onion straws starter ($8), they are a tad greasy but addictively delicious. As my grandmother used to say, "something's repeatin' on me."

Greenport Harbor Brewing Company (234 Carpenter Street, Greenport; 631-513-9019). The brewery is open Tues. through Sun. Tasting hours are Thurs. through Sun. from noon to 6 PM. Sample Harbor Ale, India Pale Ale, Black Duck Porter, and Summer Ale with hints of orange blossom honey.

■■■■ SHOP

Knotted Dreams Rug Gallery (471 Main Street, Greenport; 631-477-6686; www.knotteddreams .com). For handmade Oriental and Persian rugs.

Doofpot (300 Main Street at Stirling Square, Greenport; 631-477-0344). Tuscany via Greenport. For packed-to-the-rafters imported Italian pottery, china, and gifts.

Lydia's Antiques (215 Main Street, Greenport; 631-477-1414). Nostalgic knickknacks at every turn. A very impressive and fun-to-browse antiques shop in the heart of town. For fine antiques, advertising collectibles, vintage pottery, fine china, costume and original jewelry, and new artisan crafts. Open daily.

Goldsmith's Electronics (138 Main Street, Greenport; 631-477-0466). Old-school electronics and unique toys for girls and boys.

Greenport Tea Company (119A Main Street, Greenport; 631-477-8744; www.greenportteacompany.com). Tea for two. For libations on the steeped side. Specialty teas loose or by the bag, teapots, and kitchen supplies. High tea and a light lunch menu are served as well.

S. T. Prestons & Sons (102 Main Street, Greenport; 800-836-1165; www.prestons.com). For all things nautical: navigational instruments, mini lighthouses,

artwork, and home decor with a maritime motif (just don't overdo it.). A staple in Greenport since 1955. Open daily. If you can't make it to the fun-to-browse store, visit their online catalog.

Arcade Department Store (14 Front Street, Greenport; 631-477-1440). The name is so appropriate for this old-time variety store—there's a little something for everyone, including Greenport-themed souvenirs, holiday decorations, postcards, and greeting cards, clothes for men, women, and children, garden supplies, and health and beauty aids. I'm six-foot-six, and they've got jeans that fit me! That's no easy task. Better than a mall and more fun!

Burton's Book Store (43 Front Street, Greenport; 631-477-8536). A quaint little Main Street—style bookstore with a nice selection of Long Island-themed titles.

Metal Monk (110 Front Street, Greenport; 631-757-0232). Unique

Wares on display at Lydia's Antiques

Greenport Dock

handcrafted jewelry and métiers d'art home decorations.

▮▮▮▮ SPECIAL EVENTS

June through November: **Greenport Gallery Walk** offers an evening stroll and some beautiful local art along Greenport Gallery Row the third Sat. of every month. Visit www.greenport gallerywalk.com.

Mid-September: Greenport East End Seaport Museum & Marine Foundation hosts an annual **Maritime Festival**.

▮▮▮▮ AFTER DARK

Village Cinema (211 Front Street, Greenport; 631-477-8600). The place in town to take in a first-run summer blockbuster.

▮▮▮▮ OUTSIDE

Orient Beach State Park (Route 25, Orient; 631-323-2440; www .nysparks.state.ny.us). A pristine rocky beach for swimming, biking, and hiking along Gardiners Bay, the body of water located between the two Forks. Open year-round. Use your Empire Passport in season.

Cross Sound Ferry (Route 25, Orient; 631-323-2525; www.long islandferry.com). Provides car and passenger ferry service from Orient Point to New London, Connecticut. The boat ride takes about one hour and 20 minutes.

▮▮▮▮ WATERFRONT

Shelter Island and **Shelter Island Ferry**. From the Greenport dock, one could while away the day watching the Shelter Island ferry venture back and forth on its 15-minute trip from Greenport and back—or you can just hop on board for an inexpensive mini seafaring adventure. Once there Shelter Island offers a number of restaurants, accommodations, historical house tours, and the

2,000-plus acre Mashomack Preserve. North Ferry Company (631-749-0139) offers dozens of daily departures. Fees cost about $13 round-trip for driver and vehicle; $2 for foot passengers. South Ferry Company (631-749-1200) offer access to Sag Harbor on the South Fork as well. Also visit www.shelter-island.org.

∎∎∎∎ DRIVING TIPS

If you are skipping the North Fork vineyards and are heading straight into Greenport, save a little travel time and take Route 48 east, which will bypass a busy stretch of Route 25.

∎∎∎∎ STAY

Soundview Inn & Restaurant (Route 48, Greenport; 631-477-1910; www.soundviewinn.com). A short drive from downtown Greenport, all of Soundview's rooms are located on a private beach that faces the beautiful Long Island Sound. Swimming pool and restaurant on premises. High-season rates start at about $190 a night.

The Bartlett House B&B (503 Front Street, Greenport; 631-477-0371; www.barletthouseinn.com). A comfy 10-room B&B in a completely restored house that dates to 1908. All rooms come with private bath. It's a five-minute walk from either the LIRR train station or the downtown core and har-

bor. High season rates start at about $175 a night.

∎∎∎∎ LIRR OPTION/ LOCAL TAXI INFO

Laaaast stop! Greenport station is the last stop on the LIRR's Ronkonkoma branch. The station is quite close to the village—perhaps a 10-minute scenic stroll away. Maria's Taxi (631-477-0700) offers local cab service.

∎∎∎∎ FYI

According to the Village of Greenport's official Web site, in its illustrious maritime past dating to pre-Revolutionary War times, Greenport was once known as Winter Harbor, then Stirling, then Greenhill, and finally Greenport in 1838.

∎∎∎∎ READS AND RESOURCES

The *Suffolk Times* is a North Fork weekly. Visit www.suffolktimes .com.

Visit the **Village of Greenport** at www.greenportvillage.com.

Visit **Greenport Guide** at www.greenportonline.com.

∎∎∎∎ NEXT STOP

Compare the North Fork to the South Fork with a trip on the ferry to Sag Harbor and the Hamptons (see Chapter 21).

9 • TAKING FLIGHT IN GARDEN CITY: *Cradle of Aviation Museum*

Garden City, Mineola, Carle Place, Westbury, East Meadow, Hempstead

Fasten your seatbelts, please!

The Cradle of Aviation Museum takes to the skies with a thorough and colorful interactive look at Long Island's rich aerospace industry. Eight chronological exhibition galleries tell the tale of aviation from the Montgolfier brothers' first balloon trip to man's landing on the moon and all aircraft and aviators in between. Topics cover aviation during the two world wars, the golden age of flying, the jet age, commercial aviation, and the space age.

Tom Gwynne, who has spent his whole life in the aviation industry, first as a fighter pilot and Vietnam War vet to a Grumman employee who worked on the Apollo program, seems to have found his "retirement" dream job as acting communications director.

Gwynne says that of the 73 centerpiece aircraft and spacecraft displayed "almost all have a story behind them." And that's what makes the visit so special. In addition to the aircraft, hundreds of aviation-themed memorabilia and photos are displayed.

"The curatorial focus is on Long Island's aerospace heritage," Gwynne said. "About 95 percent of this collection was designed, built, and flown on Long Island. The other five percent is something significant like the lunar module or the *Spirit of St. Louis* sister ship."

The visit opens with the earliest attempts at flight in the form of balloons, kites, and gliders. Gwynne says that although balloons got us airborne, it was the kite that led to modern aviation.

"You can see an airplane morph out of that technology," Gwynne said. "If you cut a kite, you get a glider."

Long Island's own Hempstead Plains gets a rightful nod as well. The area offered many advantages in the early days of aviation.

"The area was flat, at sea level. There were no mountains like there were in New Jersey and Westchester," Gwynne said. "And it was close enough to the money of New York City. It was perfect for aviators."

*Cradle of
Aviation
Museum*

A who's who of early aviators, famous and those unsung heroes, tells the real story behind the aircraft on hand. Tribute is paid to, of course, the Wright Brothers, but as well to Louis Blériot, who was the first pilot to fly solo across the English Channel from France to England in 1909. His airplane is on display.

"It's the fourth oldest airplane in the United States," Gwynne said.

Harriet Quimby, a female pilot who turned the world of aviation on a gender-bending turn-of-the-century ride, also gets proper due.

"Quimby smoked cigars, drove cars, wore pants, and flew airplanes," Gwynne said. "In 1911, women just didn't do that. But the press loved her."

Gwynne says that Quimby was the first woman to fly across the English Channel from England to France. She was a publicity dar-

ling, but she got zero press for that particular feat. Quimby's fateful flight took place April 14, 1912, the same day the *Titanic* sunk. She was killed less than three months later in a plane accident.

And then there is the Curtiss JN-4, a.k.a. the Curtiss Jenny.

Many American pilots learned how to fly in World War I in a Curtiss Jenny, says Gwynne. At the beginning of the war, the government placed an order for 5,000 of the aircraft. When the war ended a year later, there were another 3,000 aircraft still on back order. The government wound up with a bit of a surplus on their hands. For a very inexpensive price, anyone could buy an airplane.

"And that's how Charles Lindbergh started," Gwynne said. "This is Charles Lindbergh's first airplane."

The plane is indeed the original

owned by Lindbergh—his initials are carved inside. The aviator personally verified that he once owned the plane and a photo of Lindbergh next to the plane confirms the evidence.

"This is a significant airplane," Gwynne said.

Another aircraft made famous by Lindbergh gets a nod as well. On display is a sister ship of the *Spirit of St. Louis*, the plane that Lindbergh flew on the first non-stop transatlantic solo flight, which took 33½ hours, from Roosevelt Field to Paris in 1927.

"This is not a replica, it's a sister ship. It was built during the same time," Gwynne said. "The design was revolutionary."

Gwynne says that the plane on hand enjoys its own unique claim to fame. Fast-forward to the early 1950s, during the filming of *The Spirit of St. Louis* starring Jimmy Stewart. The filmmakers asked the Smithsonian Institution, where the original aircraft is housed, to borrow the plane for the film. They were politely declined. Instead, the plane housed in the Cradle of Aviation Museum doubled as the plane in the movie.

Famous aviators and planes aside, there is one exhibit display in particular that remains near and dear to Gwynne's own family. The display is of a bright orange test pilot jumpsuit with mask. Upon closer inspection, the accompanying placard states that the uniform indeed belonged to Gwynne himself.

"My wife was glad to get that stuff out of the house," he quips.

The visit also offers a look at Long Island's current state of commercial aviation. Gwynne says that although the major companies such as Grumman have departed, some 250 aviation parts manufacturers remain on Long Island. The major New York City/Long Island airports provide another source of industry pride, serving millions of passengers every year. And the Cradle of Aviation Museum adds to the tally, too—some 50,000 schoolchildren visit every year.

Gwynne says that many of the docents who volunteer at the Cradle of Aviation Museum also worked on the original lunar module.

"In all, 12 people walked on the moon," he said. "We didn't find gold, we didn't find oil. So was it worth the trip?"

Gwynne says yes.

"The perspective that we actually live in a spaceship was something that became obvious," Gwynne said. "We have so many consumables and limited resources, it would behoove us to take care of the planet. So with a visit to outer space, you start to see the rise of the environmental movement. I think that may be the lasting treasure that came out of those trips. I think that perspective can be extremely valuable."

▪▪▪ INFO

Admission to the Cradle of Aviation costs $9 for adults; $8 for children and seniors. Galleries are open 9:30 AM—5 PM Tues. through Sun.; daily in summer. Call 516-572-4111 or visit www.cradleof aviation.org.

▪▪▪ MUSEUM ROW

The Cradle of Aviation Museum is one of four attractions currently open along **Museum Row**. The other destinations include the Nassau County Firefighters Museum, the Long Island Children's Museum, and Nunley's Carousel. The Museum of Science and Technology is a work in progress. Don't try to tackle them all in one day, but all are family friendly. Unfortunately, a discount combo pass for admittance to all four attractions is not yet available (are you listening, Museum Row?).

The **Nassau County Firefighters Museum and Education Center** offers vintage fire equipment and trucks, firefighting memorabilia, and, most important, teaches home safety to kids with topics that include BBQ safety, swimming pool safety, and fireplace safety. Admission costs about $4 for adults and $3.50 for seniors, children, and volunteer firefighters. Open Tues. through Sun. 10 AM—5 PM; daily in summer. Call 516-572-4177 or visit www.nc firemuseum.org.

The **Long Island Children's Museum** places kids front and center with hands-on exhibitions that explore everything from bricks to bubbles to backyard bugs. Admission costs $10. Open Tues. through Sun. 10 AM—5 PM; daily in summer. Call 516-224-5800 or visit www.licm.org.

Top off your Museum Row visit with a ride on the completely restored **Nunley's Carousel**. The 40-horse (and one lion) carousel was built in 1912 and was first located in the Canarsie waterfront section of Brooklyn at Golden City Park. It was moved to Baldwin in 1940 after New York City razed Golden City Park in the late 1930s to make way for what is now the Belt Parkway. It remained in Baldwin until 1995 and was in danger of being sold off piece by piece until it was purchased by Nassau County. It reopened in 2009 and makes the perfect complement to Museum Row. Hours are Tues. through Sun. Sept. through June; daily July and Aug. Rides cost $2.

■■■■ GETTING THERE

Museum Row is at Charles Lindbergh Boulevard in Garden City, adjacent to Nassau Community College. Take the Meadowbrook Parkway to exit M4 and follow the signs to Museum Row.

■■■■ ROOSEVELT FIELD MALL

Avid mall shoppers can make a day of it at **Roosevelt Field Mall**, where your shopping comes with authentic Long Island Aviation History 101. Originally the Curtiss Field airfield, the site was graced by aviator Amelia Earhart, among others, and is indeed the airstrip from which Charles Lindbergh departed for his transatlantic nonstop flight to Europe in 1927. There's a plaque to commemorate the event near the mall's Disney Store. The field was renamed in honor of Quentin Roosevelt, the youngest son of President Theodore Roosevelt and a fighter pilot who died on a combat mission over France during World War I. Roosevelt Field Mall first opened its doors in 1956 in the heart of bustling post–World War II suburbia—storied Levittown is a short 10-minute drive away.

Ah, a local's memories of Roosevelt Field Mall. I remember hitting the mall as a youngster in the 1970s when the likes of Woolworth, Gimbels, and Alexander's

once ruled this shopping mall roost—you could shop and then eat an inexpensive lunch at the Woolworth counter, and then enjoy an after-lunch cigarette, as smoking was permitted back then inside the store. And you always knew someone who worked at the mall, like my cousin Tommy, who short-ordered at said Woolworth counter. My best friend Jen had a stint at a number of mall eateries as well (remember Lums?).

In the days before you had a car, you got to Roosevelt Field via the N-24 bus from the Mineola terminal. I once spotted a celebrity at the mall with my friend Nora—actor and Garden City native Telly Savalas was circling the lot looking for a parking spot. No lollipop, but he did give a hearty smile and hello. It may just be a shopping mall (and it could be any Long Island shopping mall), but there are nonetheless some nostalgic memories and magic moments that happened at Roosevelt Field.

Recent recession aside, Roosevelt Field Mall stands as one of the most profitable and most occupied malls in the country, according to a recent *U.S. News and World Report* article. The mall enjoys a 96 percent occupancy rate. It is the largest mall in the State of New York and the eighth largest mall in the country.

Roosevelt Field currently boasts Nordstrom, Macy's, JCPenney, and Bloomingdale's as its anchor department stores, as well as another 270 specialty stores that include Coach, Abercrombie & Fitch, Banana Republic, Victoria's Secret, J. Crew, Diesel, Steve Madden, Kenneth Cole, Swatch, Restoration Hardware, and Williams-Sonoma. The mall includes a typical mall-style food court as well as sit-down eateries such as Legal Sea Foods and Houston's. The main entrance is at 630 Old Country Road in Garden City. You can also take the Meadowbrook Parkway to exit M2 West. Call 516-742-8000 or visit www.rooseveltfield.com.

▪▪▪▪ OUTSIDE

Eisenhower Park (Meadowbrook Parkway to exit M3 Stewart Avenue; access also available at Hempstead Turnpike in East Meadow; 516-572-0348; www .nassaucountyny.gov). Eisenhower Park dates to the 1920s as a park space, and was further developed in the 1940s as Salisbury Park. It was renamed after the president in 1956 and is one of the largest green spaces dedicated to sports and recreation in the New York metro area, says the Nassau County government Web site. So just what can you squeeze into 930 acres? If golf is your game, there are three 18-hole golf courses, a driving range with some 100 stalls, and two 18-hole miniature courses. If you're in for a swim, the Nassau County Aquatic Center is considered one of the best in the country. It was originally built for the 1998 Goodwill Games. In addition, there are three football fields, 17 baseball fields (mostly for softball), batting cages, 16 lighted tennis courts, four soccer fields, three playground areas, a fitness trail, an outdoor theater, a safety town that teaches kids street safety, and dozens of picnic areas that attract family reunions from near and far.

Hofstra University Arboretum and Bird Sanctuary (Hempstead Turnpike, Hempstead; www .hofstra.edu). The 238-acre campus includes a 12,000-tree arboretum, a 2-acre bird sanctuary, and specialized gardens. Open year-round dawn to dusk; bird sanctuary open midweek late mornings to early afternoons.

▪▪▪▪ EAT

Ben's Delicatessen (Country Glen Center, 59 Old Country Road, Carle Place; 516-742-3354). Just next door to Barnes & Noble, Ben's offers sit-down and takeout kosher deli specialties such as all-beef hot dogs with sauerkraut, authentic knishes, and home-style chicken soup with optional matzo ball.

LL Dent (221 Old Country Road, Carle Place across from Roosevelt Field; 516-742-0940; www.lldent .com). As I mentioned previously, don't be afraid of the strip mall. The L and L of the title stands for the two belles of this southern ball: owner Lillian Dent and her daughter and head chef Leisa. Popular menu delicacies include fried chicken or catfish ($14.95), as well as plenty of tasty southern sides such as collard greens with smoked turkey ($3.75), baked macaroni and cheese ($4), and Hoppin' John—black-eyed peas and rice ($3.50). Open Tues. through Sat. for lunch and dinner; Sun. for a popular brunch.

Fortune Chinese Restaurant (477 Old Country Road, Westbury; 516-333-8686).

Whereas P.F. Chang's China Bistro at the Mall at the Source (a two-minute drive east from Roosevelt Field along Old Country Road) offers a more busy chain-style restaurant feel, Fortune Chinese Restaurant just across the street outdoes its Asian neighbor with a much calmer atmosphere and more authentic creative cuisine such as breaded jumbo shrimp with Grand Marnier and a generous heaping of perfectly sautéed bok choy.

Jane Café & Restaurant (92 Main Street, Mineola; 516-742-0031). For Korean hot pot and Japanese sushi and sashimi. The beef dumplings and shrimp tempura truly satisfy for starters. Complete the meal with an order of bibim bap—a sizzling Korean hot pot of vegetables, beef, spicy bean paste, and topped with a fried egg. The tables are a bit cozy—it's easy to spy on your neighbor's fresh salmon and salad bento box and make a mental note to order it the next time you visit. The beverage of choice: a cold OB Korean lager beer (say o-bee—it stands for Oriental Brewery). The waitstaff aims to please. Open daily for lunch, dinner, and take-out. Entrées from about $10-$16.

Café Rossini (106 Main Street, Mineola; 516-877-7850). The space is nothing to look at, but the Italian fare is always consistently good. Monday night is pasta night—about $7.95 for pasta entrées such as penne Siciliana with fried eggplant, tomato sauce, and ricotta. Wednesday night is pollo fest—chicken entrées such as chicken alla zingara with artichoke hearts, red roasted peppers, white wine sauce, and mozzarella cost about $9.95 with salad and dessert. Excellent pizza topped with inventive ingredients by the pie or slice, to stay or to go. For you out-of-towners, try a Grandma slice—think a thinner-crust Sicilian.

Station Plaza Coffee Shop (206 Station Plaza North at the Mineola LIRR train station; 516-746-5150). Owner Nick and family have run the Station Plaza Coffee Shop for some three decades. For morning coffee, corn muffins, fried-egg-and-bacon sandwiches, and afternoon deluxe cheeseburger platters. You'll be served by a slew of seasoned professionals. Parking is at a premium.

Majors Steak House (284 East Meadow Avenue, East Meadow; 516-794-6600). The epitome of a casual neighborhood steak house, busy Majors gets big points for atmosphere, solid friendly service, moderate prices, and consistent steaks, burgers, and chops—always loving the two perfectly cooked grilled pork chops and applesauce, mashed potatoes, and creamed spinach. The pot of pickles and hot peppers on every table is a nice touch, too. Another location in Woodbury (8289 Jericho Turnpike, 516-367-7300). Both open daily for lunch and dinner.

▮▮▮▮ SHOP

Barnes & Noble (Country Glen Center, 91 Old Country Road, Carle Place; 516-741-9850). Travel west

from Roosevelt Field Old Country Road entrance just past the intersection of Old Country and Glen Cove Roads to this open and airy two-floor Barnes & Noble bookstore.

As Seen on TV Store (1504 Old Country Road, Westbury; 516-228-0303). Venture east of Roosevelt Field Mall to the Mall at the Source. Once there, the As Seen on TV store offers everything from Magic Jack brand telephone computer jacks to Slap Chop mini vegetable choppers, Space Bag inflatable storage containers to ShamWow cloths. You've died and gone to infomercial heaven.

Willis Hobbies (300 Willis Avenue, Mineola; 516-746-3944; www.willishobbies.com). In keeping with the kid-at-heart theme, Willis Hobbies has been fulfilling childhood fantasies for some six decades. Shop there for radio-controlled cars; trains in G, O, HO, and N scales; and model ship and airplane kits.

▮▮▮▮ SIGHTSEE

African American Museum (110 North Franklin Street, Hempstead; 516-572-0730). Highlights the heritage of African Americans through permanent and temporary exhibitions and special events. The space also provides resources through the African Atlantic Genealogical Society.

Garden City Hotel

Open Wed. through Sun. Free admission.

■■■■ SPECIAL EVENTS

Early May: **Long Island Marathon** (www.thelimarathon.com).

Early May: Museum Row Family Festival.

Summer: Eisenhower Park Ethnic Festivals and Lakeside Theatre Free Summer Concert Series (www.nassaucountyny.gov).

Mid-October: Long Island Auto Show at Nassau Coliseum.

Late October: Long Island Fall Home Show at Nassau Coliseum.

Mid-November: International Great Beer Expo at Nassau Coliseum.

■■■■ AFTER DARK

The Leroy R. & Rose W. Grumman IMAX Dome Theater at the Cradle of Aviation Museum presents original IMAX productions and the occasional Hollywood blockbuster formatted for an IMAX viewing. Classic IMAX films cost about $8.50 for adults and $6.50 for children (2–12). Hollywood versions cost $13.50 for adults; $11.50 for children. See address listed above.

Nassau Veterans Memorial Coliseum (1255 Hempstead Turnpike, Hempstead; 516-794-9300; www.nassaucoliseum.com). Home to four-time Stanley Cup champions the New York Islanders (www.islanders.nhl.com). Islander home game tickets are about $19–105. The Coliseum also attracts big-name musical acts and family-themed events such as ice shows. Tickets available through Ticketmaster (www.ticketmaster.com) or in person at the box office.

■■■■ DRIVING TIPS

Gridlock! Yes, that is an 11-lane intersection (heading west) at the corner of Glen Cove and Old Country Roads. Looking for a Black Friday bargain the day after Thanksgiving at Roosevelt Field Mall? Be prepared to get stuck in traffic.

▮▮▮▮ STAY

Garden City Hotel (45 Seventh Street; Garden City; 516-747-3000; www.gardencityhotel.com). The Garden City Hotel dates to 1874. Today the space offers some 280 upscale rooms. Rates start at about $265 a night.

Hampton Inn Garden City (1 North Avenue, Garden City; 866-539-0036; www.hamptoninn .com). A less expensive option near Roosevelt Field. Rates start at about $135 a night.

▮▮▮▮ LIRR OPTION/ LOCAL TAXI INFO

For Roosevelt Field and the Cradle of Aviation Museum, take the LIRR to the Mineola train station. LI Checker Cab of Mineola 516-746-4666) provides service to the Cradle of Aviation Museum for about $8 (for one person).

▮▮▮▮ FYI

Before his untimely death on Aug. 16, 1977, Elvis Presley was to have performed his next big arena concert Aug. 22, 1977—at the Nassau Coliseum.

▮▮▮▮ READS AND RESOURCES

The Spirit of St. Louis is Billy Wilder's 1957 quintessential tale of Lindbergh's transatlantic flight from Long Island to Europe starring Jimmy Stewart.

▮▮▮▮ NEXT STOP

Need more aeronautics? Visit the American Airpower Museum in Farmingdale (see Chapter 19).

SUBURBAN
SEASCAPES

10 • BLISSFUL MEMORIES OF JONES BEACH

Ask an expert for their professional view of Jones Beach? No thanks. Everyone who knows Long Island—particularly Jones Beach—is their own expert on this wonderful resource. This story comes from within.

If you indeed ask me my favorite thing of all about Long Island, it would have to be Jones Beach. The reasons equally range from its pristine beauty to the nostalgic memories etched in your mind no matter how far away from home you get.

My first memories of Jones Beach begin at a very early age. The summer Tuesday ritual (when Williston Park Pool was closed for its weekly cleaning), saw the Howells, the Babors, and the Georges—two carloads, three moms, and nine or so kids—off to a day at the beach. The trip, of course, was accompanied by a bounty of food, a variety of plastic and Styrofoam coolers, and an assortment of mismatched beach blankets, folding chairs, and umbrellas. We appeared on the West End 2 sands like three clans of suburban nomads in search of

an oasis by the ocean.

En route to the beach the radio station of choice was 77 WABC. It was always a kicker when the thermostat started to climb and it reached "77 WABC degrees." The Jackson 5 sang *ABC* and, although I didn't understand it at the time, Freda Payne lamented about her tarnished *Band of Gold.* If you liked the song, and were lucky, the station would play it twice: "instant replay, instant replay, instant replay..." When you saw the Jones Beach water tower, a.k.a. "the pencil," whether traveling via the Meadowbrook or Wantagh Parkways, you knew you had arrived.

For this early '70s gang, the place to be and be seen was indeed Parking Field 2. But the walk from the parking lot to the beach with all that gear took f-o-r-e-v-e-r. Mysteriously, the walk from the beach back to the car at the end of the day took even longer. Unfortunately, Parking Field 2 lay victim to the recent recession as it remained closed for the 2009 season.

The day proved easy. Activities

included relax in the sun, go for a swim, ride those rough-and-tumble waves, occasionally drink a bit of the Atlantic Ocean, bury someone in the sand, eat a slightly gritty baloney sandwich, and repeat. However, all of those outdoor adventures came with a price. In a word: sunburn. And

Lido Golf Club

Jones Beach

lots of it. Deep crimson head-to-toe sunburn. Consider back then that the word sunscreen hadn't entered the popular lexicon. The treatment of choice was a generous slathering of Noxzema to deaden the pain. You fell asleep rocking to the crashing waves and to the sting of the sunburn on your back and the potent cream in your nostrils.

But the salt water would also do a body good. Have a cut or scrape or poison ivy? My next-door neighbor, Mr. Portelli, would always say to go to the beach, go into the salt water. He was right. That Atlantic Ocean salt water would soothe any itch that ailed you.

As teens, we'd ditch our parents and make a summer day of it as well. But we were too cool for umbrellas and would again bake in the hot summer sun. We'd opt for the shorter walk to the beach available at Parking Field 6, but so did everyone else. It still remains the first lot to fill up. If you're not there by 9 AM, forget about it. We late arrivals would u-turn to our second alternative, the busier Parking Field 4.

Sometimes we'd go back at night to catch a concert at the Jones Beach Theater as it was simply called back then sans the Tommy Hilfiger or Nikon corporate moniker. Eighties stars ruled the summer stage, the likes of Sinéad O'Connor, New Order, and the most memorable concert of all performed by Squeeze, who bravely performed in the pouring rain without getting electrocuted. We were soaked to the bone, fingers pruned as if we just emerged from a bathtub full of salt water, giddy from the music and what we smoked in the parking lot just before the show. I think that concert remains as a defining nostalgic moment of my generation of Long Islanders.

A decade later saw a reverse commute out east. Commuting to Suffolk County to work via the L.I.E. in the morning meant an out-of-the-way but a much more relaxed drive home along Ocean Parkway. An after-work decompression meant a jog along the beach. And on those weekday evenings you practically had the beach all to yourself. I'd often park the car, again at Field 6, and head east for a 2-mile run, the salt spray filling my nostrils and cleansing my lungs. This would be a barefoot run along the oceanfront where firm wet sand met surf. The end-of-jog reward was a dip in the ocean—and, with no one around, often a skinny-dip. The walk-back cool-down offered a reflective pause and a stunning sunset to boot.

Although I have moved

Upstate, I visit Long Island all the time. And Jones Beach is always on my itinerary no matter what the season. But summer...a Long Island summer is synonymous with a day at that beautiful beach.

My favorite Jones Beach snapshot depicts my nephew Bobby and me, unintentionally paired in almost matching swim trunks, emerging laughing from the lively surf. I'm sure we were comparing notes about bodysurfing a recent Atlantic Ocean wave and its eventual baptism. It epitomizes the lazy days of the season and reminds me that a very good day under the sweet Long Island summer sun was had by all.

Those are some of my favorite memories of Jones Beach. What are yours?

▮▮▮▮ INFO

Parking costs about $8 per carload or use your Empire Passport. Jones Beach is open daily. Peak fees are collected mid-May through mid-Sept. 6 AM–6 PM weekends and holidays and 8 AM–4 PM weekdays. A reduced admission of $6 is charged from early April through mid-May and from mid-Sept. through early Nov.

Jones Beach also offers pool bathing at the West Bathhouse, a mini golf, and an 18-hole par-3 golf course. Call 516-221-1000. A few Web sites are devoted to Jones Beach, including www.nys parks.state.ny.us; www.jones beach.com; and www.jonesbeach .org.

■ ■ ■ ■ GETTING THERE

To get to Jones Beach take the Meadowbrook Parkway or Wantagh Parkway south and keep going—you can't miss it. It's also accessible from the east on Ocean Parkway.

■ ■ ■ ■ JONES BEACH FUN FACTS

Jones Beach was named after Major Thomas Jones, a one-time privateer who owned a large swath of property in the Massapequa area in the early 1700s.

Jones Beach was developed by Robert Moses. It was his first major public project as a master builder of the Long Island and New York City parks system and highway infrastructure.

Jones Beach officially opened Aug. 4, 1929.

Today, Jones Beach attracts some six million visitors every year.

■ ■ ■ ■ OUTSIDE

Lido Golf Club. (255 Lido Boulevard, Long Beach; 516-889-8181). It's tee time near the beach. Lido Beach Gold Club offers an 18-hole course. About $42 for guests. Dis-

counts for Long Beach and Town of Hempstead residents and 9-hole play.

■ ■ ■ ■ PERFORMANCE

Jones Beach Theater (in Wantagh, just follow the signs once you get near Jones Beach). Officially Nikon at Jones Beach Theater, I don't know of a single Long Islander who hasn't seen a show here over the years. The venue opened in 1952 and first offered musical theater performances. Local bandleader Guy Lombardo was a favorite fixture. Expanded in the late 1990s, today the theater holds some 15,000 seats and attracts top-name musical acts (often with top-dollar ticket prices).

■ ■ ■ ■ WATERFRONT

Long Beach Boardwalk and Beach (Access the boardwalk just south of Broadway—five blocks south of the main Park Avenue strip between Neptune Avenue in the east and New York Avenue in the west. Beach entrances are readily accessible all along the boardwalk.) Another good beach spot, Long Beach comes complete with a boardwalk full of colorful characters. It's also close to shops and dining, although parking comes at a premium. The price is a bit steeper than at Jones Beach, too: admission costs about $10 per person for those 13 and older. Season passes and multiple-admit discounts are also available. Beach season runs 9 AM–6 PM weekends from Memorial Day to the first day of summer; and then daily late June through Labor Day. Visit the city of Long Beach at www.longbeachny.org.

■ ■ ■ ■ EAT FREEPORT

It's not exactly a mile, but the **Nautical Mile** in Freeport manages to squeeze in about two dozen casual mostly seafood eateries along Woodcleft Avenue. The prime location right on the water, or at least the canal, adds to the price of your tab. The crowds and music can be young and boisterous. The seafood can be hit or miss. That said, it's summer, you want seafood, perhaps al fresco dining while wearing shorts and sandals, and maybe even some live music, too. Nautical Mile it is. Parking can be tricky on busy hot summer nights. Along the way try **Bracco's Clam and Oyster Bar** (319 Woodcleft Avenue; 516-378-6575), **Rachel's Waterside Grill** (281 Woodcleft Avenue; 516-546-0050; www.rachelswaterside grill.com), and **Nautilus Café** (46 Woodcleft Avenue; 516-379-2566; www.nautiluscafe.com).

To get to Nautical Mile from Jones Beach, hop on the Meadow-brook Parkway north to Merrick Road west. Head south on South Ocean Avenue. Make a left on Front Street and a quick right on Woodcleft Avenue. Visit www .nauticalmilemap.com.

■ ■ ■ ■ EAT LONG BEACH

Long Beach also has a number of good dining options on or near Park Avenue, all easily accessible from a short Long Beach board-walk stroll. To get to Long Beach from Jones Beach, take the Meadowbrook Parkway to Loop Parkway and turn right on Lido Boulevard.

Lido Kosher Deli Long Beach (641 East Park Avenue, Long Beach; 516-431-4411, www.lido kosherdeli.com). For fans of real kosher deli, this one's for you. The delicacies are to stay, to go, or order a treat online.

Swingbellys (909 West Beech Street, Long Beach; 516-431-3464; www.swingbellysbbq.com). Generous portions, casual atmosphere, and awesome comfort BBQ. The daily specials are belly-busting dangerous such as all-you-can-eat monster wing Mondays ($9) or juicy $1 rib Thursdays. A once-in-a-while spot if you're watching your weight. Open for lunch and dinner.

Five Guys Burgers and Fries (2 West Park Avenue, Long Beach; 516-431-1999; www.fiveguys.com).

Okay, so it's a franchise burger joint—exactly what you crave after a day at the beach.

Gino's Restaurant & Pizzeria (16 West Park Avenue, Long Beach; 516-432-8193). Two words: excellent pizza.

Fresco Crêperie & Café (150A East Park Avenue, Long Beach; 516-897-8097). For flavorful meal and delectable dessert crepes. Sample smoked salmon with mascarpone cheese and chive crepes ($9) or sweet Nutella hazelnut spread crepes (about $6).

Yummy Yummy Restaurant (153 East Park Avenue, Long Beach; 516-897-9872). Yes, yes. That's the name. Very good Chinese food to stay or for take-out.

Marvel Dairy Whip (258 Lido Boulevard, Lido Beach; 516-889-4232). Sample soft-serve ice cream after golf, beach, or a boardwalk stroll.

■ ■ ■ ■ SHOP

Jones Beach Gift Concessions (At most parking fields. Parking Field 4 is particularly good). Call me a sucker for a seaside souvenir, but they've a pretty nice selection of Jones Beach–themed T-shirts.

■ ■ ■ ■ SPECIAL EVENTS

Memorial Day Weekend: **Jones Beach Air Show.**

Early June: Annual Freeport Village **Nautical Mile Festival** (www .freeportny.com).

Fourth of July: Annual **Fireworks Spectacular** at Jones Beach (get there early).

Early August: The crowning of **Mr. and Ms. Jones Beach.**

■■■■ AFTER DARK

Majesty Casino Cruises (395 Woodcleft Avenue, Freeport; 516-777-5825). Gambling in New York State is limited to Indian reservations and video lottery terminals at some area horse tracks. How to fix the problem? Take a boat into international waters and gamble away. Majesty is now the lone floating casino in the area with two cruises daily, buffet included. The five-hour cruises depart at noon ($20) and 5:30 PM ($25). Games include poker, bingo, mini-baccarat, and slots. Departs from Freeport's Nautical Mile. Admission includes seasickness pill.

■■■■ STAY

Allegria Hotel (80 West Broadway, Long Beach; 516-889-1300; www.allegriahotel.com). Located directly on the Long Beach Boardwalk, Allegria offers new upscale beachfront accommodations and spa services. Deluxe king oceanview in-season rates start at about $329 for the night. Off-season rates drop to $229.

■■■■ DRIVING TIPS

Speed trap alert! The speed limit along Ocean Parkway near Jones Beach is indeed 30 mph. Any faster than that and proceed at your own risk.

Long Beach beach parking (make that parking in general anywhere near the boardwalk) requires a bit of patience.

■■■■ LIRR OPTION/ LOCAL TAXI INFO

Jones Beach is accessible from the Long Beach station (Long Beach branch) and a bus transfer to the N88 bus (just downstairs from the platform). The service begins weekends Memorial Day through late June and then daily late June through Labor Day. Service is also provided for concert nights at the Jones Beach Theater. From New York and Brooklyn the cost is about $16.50 round-trip (check for current LIRR prices as they go up every year!). The bus drops you off at the East or West Bathhouses or the Central Mall, Parking Field 4.

If you prefer the Long Beach boardwalk, the LIRR Long Beach train station is a reasonable nine-block walk to the boardwalk. Cross Park Avenue and head south along Edwards Boulevard.

■■■■ FYI

Towns and hamlets, incorporated villages and those not so, Nassau County boasts only two cities: Glen Cove and Long Beach.

■ ■ ■ ■ READS AND RESOURCES

Filmed at the Jones Beach Causeway is perhaps one of the most famous movie lines ever spoken. In *The Godfather,* Don Corleone's right-hand man Peter Clemenza (played by Richard Castellano) informs the about-to-be snuffed driver that he needs to take a leak off the side of the road. Shots fire, the driver is now dead, and Clemenza plain as day informs the triggerman to "Leave the gun. Take the cannoli." Now that's movie magic.

Watch *Jones Beach: An American Riviera,* directed by George P. Pozderec, a lighthearted look at the history of Jones Beach and the life of Robert Moses.

■ ■ ■ ■ NEXT STOP

A day at the beach. Then how about a night at a baseball game? Go Ducks! Go Ducks! Go Ducks! See Chapter 15.

11 • BURIED TREASURE ON FIRE ISLAND: *The Sunken Forest*

Sailors Haven, Fire Island Pines, Cherry Grove, Ocean Beach

Fire Island's Sunken Forest is not exactly buried, but it is indeed a unique ecological treasure.

The National Park Service offers free guided mile-long meandering boardwalk tours through the heart of the Sunken Forest at the Sailors Haven section of Fire Island. Ranger David Raymond leads the way.

Raymond says that Fire Island National Seashore is one of about 400 units of the National Park Service. The system covers all four corners of the United States.

"Fire Island is classified as a seashore," Raymond said. "But many are historical in nature."

Other New York metropolitan sites include Teddy Roosevelt's birthplace in New York City, his home at Sagamore Hill in Oyster Bay, the Gateway National Recreation Area that runs from Jamaica Bay in Queens to nearby Staten Island and New Jersey, and the William Floyd Estate, which is also part of the Fire Island Seashore unit.

The Fire Island National Seashore was established in 1964.

Raymond references neighboring Jones Beach, Ocean Parkway, and Robert Moses State Park, which was indeed named after Moses, who was considered the master builder of the New York state park system.

"It was always his intent to extend Ocean Parkway from where it stops at Robert Moses State Park all the way east to the end of Fire Island to Smith Point County Park. This was a project Moses considered up until the 1950s," Raymond said. "But Moses was met with opposition from two groups—the property owners and nature lovers."

Raymond says there are 17 private communities within the park. Having a four-lane highway would have probably eliminated those communities.

"That same highway would have destroyed this maritime forest where we're standing right now."

The Ocean Parkway extension never materialized.

Raymond then explains how Fire Island got its name. He says

there are three main theories that date to colonial times. Early colonial Dutch maps depict a number of Great South Bay islands near the Fire Island Inlet spelled as "Vier" Islands.

"Some speculate the English looked at a Dutch map and thought the Dutch misspelled fire."

Another theory has to do with pirates who were present in the area in the 1600s and 1700s. Raymond says that under maritime laws, when a ship wrecked onshore the contents belonged to whoever got there first.

"At the time there were no lighthouses. So the only way a captain could get their boat to port through a storm was to sail toward bonfires lit on the shore."

Land-based pirates, called "wreckers" according to the Web site, would often light their own bonfires to lure cargo ships to shore in order to steal their loot.

The final theory came from the poison ivy plant.

"In the fall the leaves turn a brilliant red," Raymond said. "Explorers may have seen the dunes with a reddish tint and thought they were on fire."

Besides poison ivy, Sunken Forest abounds with a variety of flora and fauna. It's known for three trees in particular: shad, sassafras, and holly. Wild cherry is also common, as are thick tangles of greenbrier and wild grapevines.

Wildlife includes the yellow-bellied sapsucker woodpecker, which makes a unique dot-to-dot row-upon-row pattern along the bark of the shad tree. The woodpecker taps the tree for sap and then feeds on the insects that feed on the sap. These shallow holes the woodpecker creates

Sailors Haven

Cherry Grove Post Office

quickly scab over so as not to permanently damage the tree. Resident chipmunks, squirrels, mice, turtles, deer, garter snakes, as well as the five-foot-long, fast-moving black racer snake all call the Sunken Forest home.

And don't forget about the mosquitoes. The tour stopped dead in its tracks for the group of 15 or so to generously apply bug spray. Consider yourself warned.

For a maritime forest to take root near the ocean is a rarity, says Raymond. For one, there are not many nutrients in sand, and the sand itself is abrasive to gentle plant leaves. In addition, the salt from the water in large doses is poisonous to many plants. The combination makes it difficult for anything to grow on the beach.

Slowly, when beach grass finally does take root, sand buries the grass, which eventually creates a sand dune. Usually there's only one dune. At this section of Fire Island, two dunes formed.

"And over time, a true forest was able to grow," Raymond said.

Raymond says that the holly trees, the tallest trees in the forest, will not grow taller than the dunes. If they did, they would be back in the line of salt spray and blowing sand. He adds that the sea salt does provide some benefits in the form of trace nutrients

such as magnesium, calcium, and phosphorus. The nutrients are carried along the salt spray in just the right amounts and absorbed by the leaves and roots.

"And that's where the name Sunken Forest comes from. Not because it's below sea level, but because it's between the dunes," Raymond said. "This maritime forest is quite unusual."

■ ■ ■ ■ INFO

Sunken Forest tours are free. Tours depart from the Sailors Haven Visitor Center Memorial Day through the first day of summer at 11 AM; daily summer through Labor Day at 11 AM weekdays and 11 AM and 2:30 PM weekends; and mid-Sept. through late Oct. weekends at 11 AM. Call 631-597-6183 (in season) or visit www.nps.gov/fiis.

■ ■ ■ ■ GETTING THERE

For the Sayville Fire Island Ferry take the L.I.E. to exit 59, Ocean Avenue South in Oakdale. Continue to Lakeland Avenue, then Railroad Avenue, turn left on Main Street in Sayville, and follow the signs for the ferry.

■ ■ ■ ■ FIRE ISLAND FERRY SERVICE

Sayville Ferry Service (41 River Road, Sayville; 631-589-0810) provides Sunken Forest/Sailors Haven, Fire Island Pines, Cherry Grove, and Water Island passenger ferry service. Round-trip fare costs about $14 and is worth every penny for the mini-cruise view alone. Parking costs $11.

Fire Island Ferries (99 Maple Avenue, Bay Shore; 631-665-3600; www.fireislandferries.com) provides ferry service from Bay Shore to all of Fire Island's western communities including Kismet, Saltaire, Fair Harbor, Atlantique, and Ocean Beach to name a few. Round-trip fare from Bay Shore to Ocean Beach costs about $17. Fri. and weekend parking costs $14 a day.

Fire Island Water Taxi (631-665-8885; www.fireislandwatertaxi.com) also provides service to and from the Long Island "mainland" to Fire Island, as well as offering lateral taxi hops by boat between all the Fire Island communities.

▪▪▪▪ FIRE ISLAND PINES/CHERRY GROVE

Fire Island Pines is a 15-minute walk along the beach east of Sailors Haven. Cherry Grove is one beach town farther east. The Pines and Cherry Grove offer a decidedly gay and lesbian feel, but all are welcome.

Accommodations include the glamorous Venetian-style Belvedere Guest House (Ocean Walk, Cherry Grove; 631-597-6448; www.belvederefireisland.com), a Cherry Grove staple for decades. Two-night minimum weekend summer stays $450–800. Newer, more modern accommodations are available at Madison Fire Island Pines (631-597-6061; www.themadisonfi.com).

Very good Pines dining options, which offer a little something for everyone, include Cherry Lane Café (631-597-7859; www.cherrysonthebay.com), Floyd's (631-597-9663) and Cherry Grove Pizza (631-597-6766).

▪▪▪▪ SPECIAL EVENTS

Fire Island firecracker. Who says you can't show up on Fire Island after Labor Day? The **Miss Fire Island Contest** (631-597-6600; www.missfireisland.com) has been turning heads at the Ice Palace since 1966. The contest is traditionally held the Saturday after Labor Day. The Coronation Ball ($35) is held the following Sunday afternoon. An Entertainer of the Year prize (entertainer as in lip-syncing drag queen) is also awarded.

▪▪▪▪ AFTER DARK

The **Ice Palace** at the **Grove Hotel** (Cherry Grove; 631-597-6600) has been a Fire Island late-night fixture for decades. The Grove Hotel also offers accommodations as well and a popular weekend tea dance.

■ ■ ■ ■ OCEAN BEACH

Ocean Beach is the largest community on Fire Island. It's home to many private residences as well as restaurants, hotels, bars, and even a movie theater. Above all, it features plenty of Atlantic Ocean beachfront. And for a diplomatic take on what was mentioned before for the Pines and Cherry Grove, although Ocean Beach offers a decidedly "straight" feel, all are welcome.

Accommodations include the boutique **Palms at Ocean Beach** (168 Cottage Walk; 631-583-8870; www.palmshotelfireisland.com); and **Clegg's Hotel** (478 Bayberry Walk; 631-583-9292; www.cleggs hotel.com), a mainstay since 1946.

Good Ocean Beach dining options include the **Hideaway Restaurant** (Bay Walk; 631-583-8900); **Rachel's Bakery and Restaurant** (325 Bay Walk; 631-583-5953); and **Michael's Ristorante and Pizzeria** (786 Evergreen Walk; 631-583-7858; www .michaels-ristorante.net).

■ ■ ■ ■ WATERFRONT

Robert Moses State Park (631-669-0470; www.nysparks.state .ny.us). You can still enjoy the beautiful Fire Island beach landscape at its westernmost point while passing on the ferry. Robert Moses State Park offers a well-maintained and quiet Atlantic Ocean beach option. To get there take the Southern State Parkway near West Islip or Bay Shore to the Robert Moses Causeway south, which offers a pretty spectacular view of the Great South Bay. Access is also accessible from Ocean Parkway if you're an age-phyrophobic (have a fear of bridges). Parking costs $8 or use your Empire Passport.

■ ■ ■ ■ SIGHTSEE

The **Fire Island Lighthouse** (Robert Moses State Park, Field 5; 631-661-4876; www.fireisland lighthouse.com). A half-mile scenic boardwalk stroll leads to the Fire Island Lighthouse, which dates to 1858. The landmark is cared for independently by the Fire Island Lighthouse Preservation Society. Tower tours and climbs ($6) offer a great view of Fire Island and the Atlantic Ocean. Guided evening tours are held throughout the year. Open daily Apr. through mid-Dec.; weekends during winter.

■ ■ ■ ■ PARKING TIPS

The ferry lots in Bay Shore and Sayville fill up fast. Friendly staff is usually on hand to help find a spot, but expect to wait in line if not catching the earliest of ferries.

■ ■ ■ ■ LIRR OPTION/ LOCAL TAXI INFO

Sailors Haven, Fire Island Pines, and Cherry Grove are accessible from the Sayville station (Montauk branch). Colonial Limo and Taxi (631-589-3500) provides area taxi service.

Ocean Beach is accessible from the Bay Shore station (Montauk branch). Tommy's Taxi (631-665-4800) offers area service.

■ ■ ■ ■ READS AND RESOURCES

Visit Fire Island, New York Travel Guide at www.fireisland.com.

The **Fire Island Ferries** Web site, www.fireislandferries.com, is another great local resource.

■ ■ ■ ■ NEXT STOP

Create your own Long Island Lighthouse Challenge. See Chapter 20.

12 • ANCESTRAL RHYTHMS IN THE HAMPTONS: *The Shinnecock Powwow*

Shinnecock, Southampton, Noyak, Sag Harbor, Bridgehampton, East Hampton, Amagansett

The Hamptons and Long Island's South Fork juxtapose the ancient traditions of the Shinnecock Nation and a celebrity-spotting summer playground for the rich and famous.

How to become a Long Island A-lister? Buy yourself a fancy oceanfront summer property, enter your horse in the Bridge-hampton Classic, and join a private beach club where the parking lot boasts the likes of BMWs, Mercedes-Benzes, and a Bentley or two—no cash for clunkers here.

How to get back to your native ancestral roots? Pay a visit to the annual Shinnecock Powwow, a Labor Day tradition located just next door—and a world away. Here's how to enjoy both.

▪▪▪▪ SHINNECOCK POWWOW

Shinnecock native Beverly Jensen, who also goes by the name Bevy Deer, which was given to her by her grandmother, is the communications director for the Shinnecock Nation and a powwow committee member. She says the Shinnecock Powwow has been going on for a very long time.

"Since time immemorial," she said. "It's what native people did and still do. It's a form of celebration."

Jensen says the Shinnecock Nation celebrates a number of annual events such as the arrival of the seasons, the Green Corn Dance, which offers a New Year's time of reflection, and even a second but private powwow held earlier during the year. The Labor Day Powwow, which is open to the public, was revived just after World War II by a number of Shinnecock members.

Besides the dozens of vendors who sell traditional crafts and food, one of the highlights of the Powwow, and an audience favorite, is the Grand Entry. It is simply a stunner to see. There are usually six of the processions held over the four-day Powwow: an opening at 7 PM on the Friday of the event, one each at around noon and 7 PM on the weekend, and the final Grand Entry at noon on Labor Day Monday, which closes the event.

The procession starts to the beat of a drum. Slowly, members of many nations make their way around a half circular natural grass stage. Dressed vibrantly in feathers and face paint, each dancer wears more bright regalia than the next.

"The regalia specifically represents a certain tribe," Jensen said. "They are different for each tribe. For example a Shinnecock would not wear the clothing of a Seminole."

The tribes come from near and far. Local nations include the Montauk and Mattinicock nations of Long Island and the Oneida and Onondaga nations of New York State. Those who traveled across the country to attend a recent Shinnecock Powwow include members from the Aztec, Arawak, Chippewa, Pueblo, Hopi, and Yakama nations. In all, more than 56 tribes were represented. All age ranges were represented, too. Youngsters and proud elders danced side by side as this grand tradition was passed from one generation to the next.

Visitors and guests are requested to follow Grand Entry etiquette. For example, hats or caps should be removed in the presence of the sovereign tribal flags and the U.S. flag as well.

"We really take a lot of pride in the flag of the motherland and the flags of our nations," Jensen said. "We also honor the U.S. veterans who defend the motherland."

That means no hats should be worn during their dedication as well. During a ceremony when an eagle feather is blessed, photography is prohibited.

The Grand Entry procession

Whaling Museum, Sag Harbor

Shinnecock Powwow

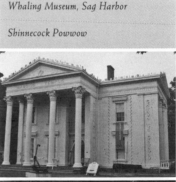

begins so that the hundreds of dancers emerge from an easterly direction. The line, which moves slowly—each step is timed to the beat of a drum—makes its way past the crowd at arm's length so the audience can get a close-up look. Once onstage, the lead dancers and flag bearers congregate in a central point. The dancers that follow make their way up on the stage and gradually move in a clockwise direction around the leads. The procession builds from the inside out, taking on a life of its own, like an ever-expanding colorful cosmos. It's one of the most hypnotic and beautiful things you will ever see.

As a dancer in the Grand Entry, Jensen says it's as thrilling to be a part of the procession as it is to see it.

"It's just spectacular."

Jensen says the powwow is most definitely a family affair. The event is a nonalcoholic one at that.

"We do our best to make our guests and visitors comfortable," Jensen said. "We want them to have fun. And we want people to remember us."

As with any celebration, food is a big part of the festivities. On the menu: clam chowders, buffalo sausage, frogs' legs, Shinnecock oysters, and fry bread, a dough patted down into a circle shape that is then dropped in hot oil until it puffs. One of Jensen's particular favorites is made by a visiting vendor and friend who "sells the most delicious buffalo sandwiches—buffalo, peppers, onions, fry bread. It's *wonderful*!"

"The powwow is always a happy time for us," Jensen said.

■ ■ ■ ■ GETTING THERE

The Shinnecock Reservation is just south of Montauk Highway near Tuckahoe Lane (not Tuckahoe Road).

■ ■ ■ ■ HAMPTONS DRIVE TOUR

Here is a suggested Hamptons and South Fork driving tour that offers a nice introduction to the area if you've never been. That said, this may be a difficult endeavor during the peak summer season. Why? In a word: traffic. And lots of it. The tour starts in Noyak and Sag Harbor, continues southeast through East Hampton and Amagansett, and then backtracks to Bridgehampton and Southampton. Restaurant, lodging, shopping, and sightseeing suggestions are grouped within each town. Be prepared to shell out some cash, as accommodations don't come cheap.

■■■■ SAG HARBOR

On Route 27/Sunrise Highway heading east, about 4 miles past the Shinnecock Canal, you'll see a sign, a left turn, for Sag Harbor. Take it. You're now on County Road 38. It's the less-traveled way to get to Sag Harbor. It takes us to our first stop.

Elizabeth A. Morton National Wildlife Refuge (784 Noyack Road, Sag Harbor; 631-286-0485; www.fws.gov/northeast/long islandrefuges). A must for bird-watchers and nature photographers. This amazing tranquil 187-acre walk in the woods teems with a variety of indigenous bird species. Add some birdseed to the palm of your hand, stand still as a statue, and you might just make some new feathered friends. Short nature trails lead to the Jessups Neck Peninsula, which separates the Little Peconic and Noyack Bays. Access is by honor system of leaving $4 in an envelope. Unfortunately, they often run out of envelopes. Wrap your cash in a piece of paper, drop it in the box, and you're good to go. It's operated by the U.S. Fish and Wildlife Service. Continue along County Road 38 into Sag Harbor.

Sag Harbor Main Street—style shopping is fun to buy and browse. Visit **BookHampton** (20 Main Street; 631-725-8425; www .bookhampton.com), a charming little bookstore. There are four South Fork stores in all; also in Southampton, East Hampton, and Amagansett. **Beach Bungalow** (26 Main Street; 631-725-4292) offers tasteful beach-inspired home decor and original designs. **Our Gig Two** (56 Main Street; 631-725-0065) is a place for fun antiques and jewelry. **Sag Harbor Variety Store** (45 Main Street; 631-725-9706) is an old-school five-and-dime store with everything under the sun, including a dose of nostalgia. **Kites of the Harbor** (75 Main Street, 631-725-9063) boasts kites in all shapes, sizes, and every color of the rainbow.

Dining options abound in Sag Harbor as well. **New Paradise Café** (126 Main Street; 631-725-6080) highlights bistro flair and contemporary American fare. Entrées $18—37. **Sen** (23 Main Street; 631-725-1774; www.sen restaurant.com) is pricey but spot-on for sushi and Japanese cuisine. A block off the Main Street path you'll find **Espresso— The Little Italian Market** (184 Division Street, 631-725-4433; www .espressoitalianmarket.com), for tasty Italian fare in a casual deli-style setting. Espresso offers affordable focaccia sandwiches, hot heros, pasta, and pizza—more than 100 menu items in all. (And wait, it's the Hamptons—did I say affordable? Yes!) Open for breakfast, lunch, and dinner.

There are plenty of things to see and do, too, in Sag Harbor. Sag Harbor **Old Custom House** (Main and Garden Street; 631-692-4664) highlights the home of Henry Packer Dering, Sag Harbor's first U.S. customs master. Rooms include formal dining, office, kitchen, pantry, and laundry. Visits cost $3. Open Memorial Day through Columbus Day. The **Sag Harbor Whaling and Historical Museum** (200 Main Street; 631-725-0770, www.sagharbor whalingmuseum.org) highlights the area's maritime heritage. **Sag Harbor Cinema** (90 Main Street, Sag Harbor; 631-725-0010) offers first-run film features in an old-time movie house. For live performances, **Bay Street Theatre** (Bay Street; 631-725-9500; www .baystreet.org) is a small space of 299 seats that attracts some pretty big names such as Alan Alda, Joy Behar, and Lewis Black.

Stay overnight at the elegant **American Hotel** (49 Main Street; 631-725-3535; www.theamerican hotel.com). This eight-room inn dates to 1846. Summer rates start at $250 a night weekdays; $400 weekend nights.

▌▌▌▌ EAST HAMPTON

Located east of Sag Harbor in the Springs near East Hampton, you'll find the **Pollock-Krasner House & Study Center** (830 Springs-Fireplace Road, East Hampton; 631-324-4929; www.pkhouse .org). This National Historic Landmark is the former home and studio of acclaimed abstract expressionist Jackson Pollock. He lived there with his wife, fellow artist Lee Krasner. The artists' house and studio are open Thurs. through Sat. from May through Oct. General admission costs $5. Hours are 1–5 PM Guided tours are available by appointment for $10.

LongHouse Reserve (133 Hands Creek Road, East Hampton; 631-329-3568; www.longhouse.org). With an emphasis on design, LongHouse offers a gallery space, arboretum, and a stunning sculpture garden. $10.

East Hampton Historical Society (101 Main Street, East Hampton; 631-324-6850; www.east hamptonhistory.org). The East Hampton Historical Society oversees a number of historical properties and landmarks including the Mulford Farm and Barn, the Town House, the Osborn-Jackson House, Clinton Academy, and the East Hampton Town Marine Museum. The Web site and office offers pertinent info on addresses, exhibitions and collections, and hours and fees for each.

Nick and Toni's (136 North Main Street, East Hampton; 631-

324-3550; www.nickandtonis .com). Local and fresh ingredients combine to create fine Italian specialties and grilled fare with an A-lister sensibility. For pizza ($16) and entrées from $22—38.

Guild Hall (158 Main Street, East Hampton; 631-824-0806; www.guildhall.org). Guild Hall offers museum exhibition space as well as the John Drew Theater for live performances.

The Baker House 1650 (181 Main Street, East Hampton; 631-324-4081; www.bakerhouse1650 .com). The Baker House offers refined luxurious accommodations, gardens, a pool, and spa in the heart of East Hampton. Summer rates start at $695 a night.

▪▪▪▪ AMAGANSETT

Miss Amelia's Cottage and Roy Lester Carriage Museum (Main Street, Amagansett; 631-267-3020). Built in 1725, the cottage museum ($2) pays tribute to Amagansett's colonial era. Pony rides ($5) are offered every summer. Open Late May through early Sept., Fri. through Sun.

The Stephen Talkhouse (161 Main St, Amagansett; 631-267-3117; www.stephentalkhouse .com). The informal place for excellent live music performances on the South Fork. The space is named for Montaukett native

Stephen Taukus "Talkhouse" Pharaoh. The Web site pays him a most proper hommage. Talkhouse is buried at Theodore Roosevelt County Park in Montauk.

Roadside eateries on the way to Montauk rule. For good outdoor eats and a lively vibe, try **Cyril's Fish House** (1899 Montauk Highway, Amagansett; 631-267-7993). Seafood entrées from $12—23. Cash only. Also try **Lobster Roll/Lunch** (Montauk Highway, Amagansett; 631-267-3740; www.lobsterroll .com). Entrées $17.95 and up. Closed Tues. and Wednesday.

▪▪▪▪ BRIDGEHAMPTON AND WATER MILL

Backtrack west along Route 27 past East Hampton into Bridgehampton and Water Mill. The **Bridgehampton Historical Society** (2368 Montauk Highway, Bridgehampton; 631-537-1088; www.bridgehamptonhistoricalsoc iety.org) oversees local history and treasures such as the Corwith House and Nathanial Rogers House.

Across the street, **Bridgehampton Candy Kitchen** (Montauk Highway, Bridgehampton; 631-537-9885) offers diner fare and sweet treats. **Bobby Van's** (2393 Montauk Highway, Bridgehampton; 631-537-0590; www.bobby vans.com) is a serious local steakhouse staple.

The **Water Mill Museum** (41 Old Mill Road, Water Mill; 631-726-4625; www.watermillmuseum .org) offers a seasonal dose of colonial history.

▪▪▪▪ SOUTHAMPTON

Southampton Historical Museums (17 Meeting House Lane, Southampton; 631-283-2494; www.southamptonhistorical museum.org) provides info on four local historical attractions: Rogers Mansion, Thomas Halsey Homestead, Pelletreau Shop, and Conscience Point.

Shippy's Pumpernickels Restaurant East (36 Windmill Lane, Southampton; 631-283-0007; www.shippyspumpernickels .com). A Southampton tradition since the 1950s. The generous menu offers steaks, chops, seafood, and German specialties. Open daily for lunch and dinner. Entrées $24–33.

Fine shopping abounds in Southampton Village (and East Hampton, too). The Main Street area features dozens of retailers including **Brooks Brothers** (48 Main Street; 631-287-3936); **Saks Fifth Avenue** (One Hampton Road; 631-283-3500); **Villeroy and Boch** (35 Main Street; 631-283-7172); and **Hildreth's Department Store** (515 Main Street; 631-283-2300).

▪▪▪▪ SPECIAL EVENTS

Early June: **Hamptons Home and Garden Show** (www.hhgshow .com).

Mid-July: **Hamptons Greek Festival.** For Greek dancing and delicacies (www.kimisishamptons .ny.goarch.org).

Late August–Early September: **The Hampton Classic Horse Show** in Bridgehampton (www .hamptonclassic.com).

Early October: **Hamptons International Film Festival** (www.hamptonsfilmfest.org).

▪▪▪▪ DRIVING TIPS

The South Fork is renowned for summer sun, fun—and, as mentioned earlier, traffic! Lots of it. Proceed with patience during the dog days of summer or venture out east during the off season to have the place practically to yourself. In addition, it's fun to party in the Hamptons, but please don't drink and drive.

And here's a museum tip: many of the smaller area museums are seasonal. Check operating hours at each location.

▪▪▪▪ LIRR OPTION/ LOCAL TAXI INFO

The Montauk branch of the LIRR stops throughout the Hamptons with stations in Southampton, Bridgehampton, East Hampton,

■■■■ THE HAMPTONS IN FILM AND LITERATURE

Think you've seen that tall fancy hedge before in your favorite movie? Here are some well-known works from stage, screen, and literature with a decidedly Hamptons flair.

Grey Gardens began life as a deliciously twisted voyeuristic 1975 documentary about Edith "Big Edie" Ewing Bouvier Beale and Edith "Little Edie" Bouvier Beale, Jackie O's aunt and cousin, respectively. The tale was turned into a Broadway musical of the same name in 2006, garnering Christine Ebersole and Mary Louise Wilson Tony Awards for their lead portrayals. Most recent accolades went to the HBO 2009 version starring Drew Barrymore and Emmy-winner Jessica Lange.

Pollock, a 2000 film bio of artist Jackson Pollock, garnered an Oscar nomination for actor Ed Harris in the title role. Marcia Gay Harden won the Best Supporting Actress statuette for her role as Pollack's wife Lee Krasner.

A Widow for One Year is one of novelist John Irving's finer moments. The 1998 novel follows a young student who ventures to the East End of Long Island to work for a womanizing children's book author as an assistant. This partial plot of the novel was adapted for the big screen in the equally highly recommended 2004 drama *The Door in the Floor* starring Jeff Bridges and Kim Basinger.

Love and Death on Long Island was first a 1990 novella written by Gilbert Adair. It was made into a feature film in 1997 starring John Hurt as a Brit who's obsessed with Jason Priestley's hunky actor character. Although the movie wasn't actually shot on Long Island, it's fun to imagine Hurt's character strolling the side streets of Southampton on foot, a rare occurrence in these parts.

L.I.E. is an independent film from 2001 that explores the relationship between an adolescent boy overcoming the death of his mother in a Long Island Expressway car accident and his unseemly much older male neighbor. Although it's set in mid Suffolk County, you'll no doubt pass the pivotal L.I.E. rest stops featured in the film on your way out east.

and Amagansett. McRides Taxi (631-283-1900) offers service in Southampton. Sag Harbor Car Service (631-537-7400) offers service in Bridgehampton. Amagansett Bus and Taxi (631-324-4100) offers cab service in East Hampton and Amagansett.

The **Hampton Jitney** has been shipping Manhattanites from the city to their sumptuous East End summer digs since the mid-1970s. Call 631-283-4600 or 212-362-8400. Also visit www.hampton jitney.com.

■ ■ ■ ■ FYI

The tall-growing, meticulously manicured hedge of choice in the Southamptons is the privet. Read *Privet Lives: An Imaginary Tale of Southampton's Iconic Shrub* by local landscape architect Perry Guillot.

■ ■ ■ ■ READS AND RESOURCES

The Hamptons, a Complete Guide: Including the North Fork and Shelter Island (A Great Destinations Guide) by Suzy Forbes Chase.

■ ■ ■ ■ NEXT STOP

The Hamptons runs far and wide, and you'll no doubt see the infamous Big Duck on your way here if coming via Riverhead. Have a look at nearby Westhampton and the Moriches (Chapter 21).

13 • BEACON OF HOME IN MONTAUK: *The Montauk Lighthouse*

Montauk

If ever there was a grand symbol of Long Island, the Montauk Lighthouse most definitely ranks with the best of them.

Henry Osmers has been a fan of the Montauk Lighthouse for much longer than the past nine years he has spent as a staff Montauk Lighthouse historian. For one, he travels 60 miles every day to get to the job that he adores.

"I love talking to people," he said. "And I love talking about the lighthouse."

Osmers recalls the time when his father brought him to see the Montauk Lighthouse when he was a youngster of seven years old. The young Osmers stood in the foreground when his father took a snapshot with the lighthouse in the background. Does he still have that photo?

"Oh, I certainly do," Osmers said. "It's still on the shelf in my living room."

Osmers vividly remembers the date the photo was taken: August 17, 1957. He repeated the photo op 50 years later to the day, on August 17, 2007, standing in the same spot with his wife taking the photo.

Osmers says that lighthouses aren't necessarily obsolete in this electronic age. He likens the sentiment to a sports metaphor.

"It's like a pitcher in the bull pen," he said. "You have a starting pitcher, but sometimes you need relief. GPS is fine. But suppose it crashes. Sometimes computers do. That's why this is still an active lighthouse."

The Montauk Lighthouse is the fourth oldest lighthouse in continuous operation in the United States, says Osmers. The lighthouse was commissioned by President George Washington in 1792. It was completed in November of 1796. It is currently listed on the National Register of Historic Places. Today, the lighthouse is run by the Montauk Historical Society (parking next door is New York State property).

The museum space, which is kept in pristine condition and is not to be missed, offers a thoughtful look at the history of the lighthouse and local history as well. Topics explore local ship-wrecks and famous ships, too, such as the slave ship the *Amistad,* which was apprehended by the U.S. Navy about 7 miles away.

The unique geographical attributes of the area, and its main problem of erosion, get an important nod as well. For example, in the 1960s, after decades of hurricane damage and erosion, the lighthouse was in danger of falling into the Atlantic Ocean unless it was moved. To the rescue came Giorgina Reid, an Italian immigrant savvy in the farming techniques of agriculture terracing in her native Italy.

"She proposed to the Coast Guard that the bluff at Montauk Point could be terraced, and they gave her permission to do it," Osmers said. "She spent 16 years working here until she was 77 years old."

The terracing project took some three decades, Osmers says, and was completed in 1998. A collection of photographs offers a fascinating before and after.

"She's a remarkable woman," Osmers said. "She saved the lighthouse."

Of course, a visit to the lighthouse wouldn't be complete without a climb to the top—137 steps in all.

"This area is so busy with boats," Osmers said. "And local

mariners still tell us that there's something comforting about seeing this light at night."

Osmers simply calls it a symbol of home.

"This is a place of history. It's part of America's maritime past. And it gives Long Islanders a wonderful sense of place."

▪▪▪▪ INFO

Admission to the Montauk Point Lighthouse costs $8.50 for adults, $7 for seniors, and $4 for children. Parking is available ($8) at the adjacent lot of Montauk Point State Park. The lighthouse is open daily from early May through mid-Oct. Peak summer hours are 10:30 AM—4:30 or 5:30 PM depending on the day of the week. The lighthouse is also open certain fall, spring, and holiday weekends Nov. through Apr. The Montauk Lighthouse receives from 80,000 to 100,000 visitors a year. Osmers says the Sunday before Labor Day is typically one of the busiest days of the year. Call 631-668-2544 or visit www.montauk lighthouse.com.

■ ■ ■ ■ GETTING THERE

Take the L.I.E. to exit 70. Proceed south on County Road 111, then go east on Route 27 to Montauk Point. En route to the lighthouse past downtown Montauk, you'll easily find a number of scenic overlooks that offer ample parking, spectacular views, and well-marked trails.

■ ■ ■ ■ OUTSIDE

Montauk Downs State Park (50 South Fairview Avenue, Montauk; 631-668-5000; www.montauk downs.org). Montauk's premier place for 18 holes of public golf. The course is open every day except Christmas, weather permitting. New York State resident fees range from a $24 weekday twilight tee time to a $46 fee weekends and holidays. The site also includes a driving range, pro shop, and restaurant.

Theodore Roosevelt County Park (Montauk Highway, 3 miles east of downtown Montauk; 631-852-7878; www.co.suffolk.ny.us).

Situated just west of Montauk Point State Park, the 1,150-plus-acre space includes a number of historical attributes. It's home to Montaukett Village, the home and burial grounds of the local Indian nation for which the area is named—legendary local native Steven Talkhouse is buried there. It's also home of Camp Wikoff, the quarantine camp where Theodore Roosevelt and his 28,000 Rough Riders were stationed after their 1898 return from the Spanish-American War. The space offers horseback riding, hiking, beach access, camping (for self-contained campers), and a Spanish-American War exhibition. It's also home to the Deep Hollow Ranch mentioned next.

Deep Hollow Ranch (Montauk Highway, Montauk; 631-668-2744; www.deephollowranch .com). The Wild…East? Established in 1658, Deep Hollow Ranch is considered the oldest cattle ranch in the country. For pony parties and horseback riding amid some 3,000 acres of gorgeous rolling greenery and seaside trails.

■ ■ ■ ■ SIGHTSEE

Depot Art Gallery and Art School (At Edgemere and Flamingo Roads; 631-668-5336; www .montaukartistsassociation.com). Take the former LIRR train depot and turn it into a small art gallery. The visit won't take all day, but the space, run by the Montauk Artists' Association, offers artworks created by local artists. Now that's what I call an original souvenir.

▪▪▪▪ WATERFRONT

Hither Hills State Park (Old Montauk Highway, Montauk; 631-668-2554; www.nysparks.state.ny.us). An Atlantic Ocean public beachfront park along Old Montauk Highway just before town that offers hiking trails and picnic areas. Parking fills up fast during peak summer season. Parking

Deep Hollow Ranch

costs about $8 per car or use your Empire Passport. Open year-round. On-site camping Apr. through Nov. Camping fees for New York State residents cost about $28 per night.

Viking Fishing Fleet and Ferry (462 West Lake Drive, Montauk; 631-668-5700; www.vikingfleet .com). Viking offers fishing excursions Apr. through Nov. and popular whale-watching tours Sat., Sun., and Mon. from July through about Labor Day. The 2009 season of whale-watching saw plenty of marine life including humpback, fin, sperm, and pilot whales; common and bottlenose dolphins; and hammerhead and great white sharks. About $49 for adults.

▪▪▪▪ EAT MONTAUK

Gosman's Dock (Montauk Harbor, 500 West Lake Drive, Montauk; 631-668-2447; www.gosmans .com). Gosman's offers four restaurants from a sit-down style eatery to a clam bar café, a take-out window, and a seafood market. The best part of all is the view. There's plenty of seaside seating and friendly service throughout. Open seasonally.

The Fort Pond Bay Company (www.harvest2000.com) operates two Montauk restos worthy of a visit. **Harvest on Fort Pond** (11 South Emery Street; 631-668-

5574) offers inventive seafood and pasta with dishes influenced by the Mediterranean. **East by Northeast** (51 Edgemere; 631-668-2872) adds flavors from the Orient to their Long Island seafood and produce. Both offer simple menus, fresh ingredients, and graceful atmosphere.

Dave's Grill (468 West Lake Drive, Montauk; 631-668-9190; www.davesgrill.com). Popular Dave's Grill aims to please and please it does, with seafood, pasta, and a bountiful selection of starters. Entrées $18.95—38.95. Open May through Oct. for dinner.

Inlet Seafood Restaurant (541 East Lake Drive, Montauk; 631-668-4272; www.inletseafood.com). A wise choice for seafood and sushi in Montauk. Entrées include seafood fra diavolo ($24) of shrimp, scallops, mussels, and clams smothered in a spicy marinara sauce served over linguine, and Cajun fish burritos or tacos ($18). Open daily for lunch and dinner in summer.

Montauk Bake Shoppe (The Plaza, Montauk; 631-668-2439; www.montaukbakeshoppe.com). Two words: jelly croissants. Folks line up for them. They'll even ship them to you fresh for a true taste of Montauk when you get back home. Coffee and pastries, too. Open daily Mar. through Dec.

■ ■ ■ ■ SHOP

Barnacle Books (37A The Plaza, Montauk; 631-668-4599). Just in case you need something to read at the beach.

Whoa! Nellie! (770 Main Street/Montauk Highway, Montauk; 631-238-5161; www.whoanellieretro.com). For vintage kitsch, retro fun, and nostalgic collectibles—a living breathing eBay store come to life. Also in Westhampton Beach (1 Sunset Avenue; 631-722-8509).

Sunset Surf Shack (76 South Elmwood Avenue, Montauk; 631-668-2495). A colorful surf shop for the surfboarder in you.

Plaza Surf & Sports (716 Montauk Highway, Montauk; 631-668-9300; www.plazasurfnsports.net). A well-stocked sporting goods store that sells beachwear and offers bike and moped rentals.

■ ■ ■ ■ SPECIAL EVENTS

Late May (usually Memorial Day weekend): **Montauk Fine Arts Festival**. Held outdoors at The Plaza traffic circle along Montauk Highway.

■ ■ ■ ■ AFTER DARK

Montauk Movie (3 Edgemere Street, Montauk; 631-668-2393). For first-run movies. Open Apr. through Oct.

Montauk Playhouse Community Center (240 Edgemere Street, Montauk; 631-668-1124 or 631-668-1612; www.montaukplayhouse.org). The former Montauk Playhouse is now in its first phase as a community center. It hosts the occasional live theater performance.

■■■■ DRIVING TIPS

Slow down! You'll no doubt have to drive through the likes of Southampton, East Hampton, and Amagansett on your way to Montauk along Montauk Highway (Route 27). The speed limit can range from 55 mph down to 35 mph quite quickly. That said, the peak summer traffic in the Hamptons may just keep you well under the speed limit.

Also, Route 27 in Nassau and Suffolk counties is also known as Sunrise Highway. Once in the South Fork, Route 27 eventually turns into Montauk Highway and then Montauk Point State Parkway.

■■■■ STAY

There are dozens of places to stay in Montauk. That means this chapter enjoys more hotel and motel listings than the other chapters simply because it's a destination to do just that: go to the beach, go for a swim, eat some lunch, sunbathe, turn over, go for a swim, eat dinner, repeat. We're talking serious downtime here. Here are some suggestions.

The Surf Lodge (183 Edgemere Street, Montauk; 631-238-5190; www.thesurflodge.com). Clean contemporary updated digs that take inspiration from the beach. The location leaves you quite close to the LIRR train station, but a short distance from "downtown" Montauk and the fishing charters. It's about a half mile away from the Atlantic Ocean. That said, the space does enjoy a water view on Fort Pond. I envision this as a good place if you're bringing a bicycle along on your train trip and then biking to the beach and lighthouse.

Blue Haven Motel (533 West Lake Drive, Montauk; 631-668-5943; bluehavenmotel.com). Blue Haven offers the basics and leaves you much closer to the fishing and whale-watching charters if you're in town for that type of sports adventure fun.

For accommodations directly on the Atlantic Ocean near the small downtown core, venture to South Edgewater and South Emerson avenues just south of the Plaza traffic circle along Route 27/Montauk Highway. The vicinity boasts about 15 motel-style informal digs that offer basic rooms and efficiencies. Some of these are seasonal. About half come with an ocean view—just look for ocean in the name, such as **Ocean End** (80 South Emerson Avenue; 631-668-5051); **Ocean Surf Resort** (84 South Emerson Avenue; 631-668-3332; www.oceansurfresort); and **Ocean Beach Resort** at Montauk (108 South Emerson Avenue; 631-668-4000; www.dunesresorts.com/ob). Not directly on the ocean but just across the street, **Sole East Beach** (107 South Emerson Avenue; 631-668-6700; www.soleeast.com) offers updated accommodations.

Other Atlantic Ocean beachfront properties a bit farther from the downtown area include **Gurney's Inn Resort, Spa, and Conference Center** (290 Old Montauk

Montauk scenery

Highway; 631-668-2345; www.gurneysinn.com), a popular Montauk staple since 1926; and **Hartman's Briney Breezes Motel** (693 Old Montauk Highway; 631-668-2290; www.brineybreezes.com).

Finally, if you're arriving by car—or specifically by boat, **Montauk Yacht Club Resort and Marina** (32 Star Island Road off West Lake Drive; 1-888-692-8668; www.montaukyachtclub.com) offers upscale accommodations—107 rooms and 232 marina slips in all. There is also an on-site spa, a sauna, two swimming pools, and restaurants.

■■■■ LIRR OPTION/ LOCAL TAXI INFO

The LIRR offers daily service to Montauk. The Penn Station to Montauk trip usually lasts just more than three hours. An express train headed east on Fri. and west on Sun. is offered during peak summer months. Lindy's Taxi (631-668-8888) provides area cab service.

■■■■ FYI

Eye spy. That chill in the air is coming from the Cold War. Easily viewed from atop the Montauk Point Lighthouse is a SAGE (Semi Automatic Ground Environment) AN/FPS-35 radar located in Camp Hero State Park. The long-range radar, built in 1958 at the height of the Cold War before spy satellites ruled the heavens, could detect objects up to 200 miles away. It was deactivated by 1984, cost too much money to tear down, and, in 2002, was listed on the National Register of Historic Places. It's fenced off, but you can still get a close-up view of the overpowering 80-foot monolithic concrete base and the equally impressive 40-ton antenna within Camp Hero.

∎∎∎∎ READS AND RESOURCES

Read *On Eagle's Beak: A History of the Montauk Point Lighthouse* by lighthouse historian Henry Osmers.

Also read Osmers' other book, *Living on the Edge,* which tells about life at the lighthouse from 1930 to 1945.

"It's the story of the last three civilian lighthouse keepers," Osmers said. "What makes it interesting is that they didn't get along with each other."

Read *Falvey's Guide to Fishing Long Island* by Kevin Falvey.

Visit the **Montauk Chamber of Commerce** at www.montauk chamber.com.

∎∎∎∎ NEXT STOP

The nearby North Fork's vineyards are all about good taste (see Chapter 18).

PLAY

NYRA, ADAM COGLIANESE

14 • HIGH STAKES IN ELMONT:
Belmont Park Racetrack

Elmont, Floral Park, Franklin Square

Twitter tweets, Facebook friends, YouTube videos, a daily blog, and not one, not two, but three Web sites.

This ain't your grandfather's day at the races.

Belmont Park has been providing horse racing thrills since 1905. The Belmont Stakes, the third leg of horse racing's illustrious Triple Crown, which includes the Kentucky Derby and the Preakness, dates even older than the park itself—to 1867. The event is indeed Belmont Park's most prestigious and busy event. Just how busy?

"It depends on if there's a Triple Crown opportunity," said Dan Silver, director of communications and media relations for New York Racing Authority. Silver says that without a Triple Crown horse in contention, the Belmont Stakes draws from 60,000 to 80,000 spectators. With a Triple Crown possibility on the horizon, the number jumps considerably— Belmont Park sees anywhere from 100,000 to 130,000 spectators on any given Belmont Stakes day

that boasts a Triple Crown contender.

"The Triple Crown can make or break the day," Silver said. "Whenever there's the opportunity for a Triple Crown winner, there's much more interest. To put things in perspective, I've never seen a Triple Crown winner in my lifetime."

Silver was born in 1979. The last Triple Crown winner was in 1978. The winning horse was Affirmed.

That said, to enjoy a day at the races, you don't have to wait for Belmont Stakes day. In fact, it's not the only stakes race in town— there are dozens.

"Belmont and Saratoga have more stakes racing than anywhere in the country," Silver said. "It's the best racing in the country."

So what makes for a stakes race? Here's Horse Racing 101:

There are different levels of racing, Silver says, which are broken into claiming races, allowance races, and stakes races. A claiming race basically means that any horse in the race can be purchased. The horses within that particular race are all cost comparative.

"So if you took out an owner's license from New York state, had an account at the track, and there's a $20,000 claiming race, you could buy any of the horses in the race for $20,000. In essence the horse would be for sale," Silver said. "The predominant races in America are claiming races."

The next levels up are maiden and allowance races. A maiden race means a horse has never won, and an allowance race is one step higher. Here, the horses may have won but not in the recent past. In addition, these horses are not for sale. Next are the ungraded stakes races.

"Think very good horses," Silver said.

A very small percentage of races in America are stakes races. Within that stakes category there are ungraded, grade three, grade two, and grade one races—the top level. Belmont enjoys a number of grade-one-level races. On Belmont Stakes day there are upward of five.

"The stakes races are the highest level of competition."

How did Silver learn so much about the world of horse racing? He went to school. Silver attended University of Arizona's graduate-level racetrack industry program. In fact, it's the only school in the

nation that offers the curriculum. Silver was the first student accepted into the program for the racetrack industry. He graduated in 2007 and has been with the NYRA ever since.

Silver says that the three New York—area tracks (Belmont, Aqueduct, and Saratoga) enjoy quite different demographics. Whereas the majority of spectators at most tracks around the country are older males, Saratoga is something of an anomaly. Attracting upward of 25,000 visitors a day, the six-week summer run boasts a 50/50 male-to-female ratio with many younger folks in attendance. The best horses and jockeys, a beautiful upstate summer setting, and vacationers looking to strike it rich add to the confluence of factors that make Saratoga unique. Silver aims to take a few lessons from Saratoga's distinct attendance attributes and bring them to Belmont. How does he help attract the next generation of horse racing fans? One way is with the click of a mouse.

"We're working on our online presence," Silver said.

NYRA indeed hosts a Facebook page, two Twitter pages, offers YouTube video recaps, and posts the informal behind-the-scenes *Belmont Insider Blog*.

"We're very technologically advanced," he said.

Silver adds that a day at the races also includes tips for newcomers and guides on how to bet from the basic win, place, or show bets to more exotic wagers such as the Pick 6, where you must choose the winning six horses of six races in succession. If you need a little monetary inspiration, consider that the largest payoff at Belmont was indeed a Pick 6 win in 1991. The lucky gamblers took home $727,130.

Besides the chance of a big cash payout, Belmont also offers good old-fashioned quality downtime including a beautiful backyard area full of shade trees and picnic tables where families, yes families, can bring the kids.

"We're making an effort to attract a new demographic," Silver said. "We hope that if you visit once, you'll be hooked."

That Pick 6 win would definitely help.

■■■■ INFO

Belmont Park spring and summer meets run from late Apr. through late July. Fall meets run mid-Sept. through late Oct. Grandstand admission costs $2. Parking costs $2. Belmont Stakes day admission costs $10. Parking on that day also costs $10. Call 516-488-6000. Also visit www.nyra.com and www.belmontstakes.com.

■■■■ GETTING THERE

Belmont Park is at 2150 Hempstead Turnpike in Elmont. Parking is also accessible by taking the Cross Island Parkway to exit 26D.

■■■■ EAT FLORAL PARK

There's a bit of a culinary bull's-eye in the heart of Floral Park, about a five-minute drive from Belmont Park. Almost twenty quality restaurants and inviting pubs offer a little something for everyone. It's an ethnic-inspired gastronomic trip around the world. Here's how to dine out before or after the big race.

Crabtree's Restaurant (226 Jericho Turnpike, Floral Park; 516-326-7769; www.crabtrees restaurant.com). Crabtree's pays homage to the Our Gang Little Rascals comedies in a fun understated way complete with nostalgic black-and-white photographs and memorabilia that adorn the walls. The generous menu offers inventive seafood, traditional grill, and creative Mediterranean mix for dinner; and hearty sandwiches, generous salads, and tasty grilled entrées for lunch. Start with the spot-on sumptuous deep-fried ravioli. Very friendly professional staff and a comfy courtyard come summer. Dinner entrées from $9.95–23.95. Open weekdays for lunch, daily for dinner, Sun. for brunch.

Trinity Restaurant and Bar (190 Jericho Turnpike, Floral Park; 516-358-5584; www.trinity restaurant.com). Trinity provides an affordable and relaxed bistro/pub atmosphere with an emphasis on Irish fare. Catfish fingers for starters, pot roast sandwiches for lunch, traditional lamb stew for dinner. Dinner entrées from $11.95–17.95.

Stella Ristorante (152 Jericho Turnpike, Floral Park; 516-775-2202; www.stellaristorante.com). A family-owned Floral Park staple for four decades and counting. For savory Italian specialties. Great service, too—ask for Ryan! Open for lunch Tues. through Fri., and Sun. Open for dinner Tues. through Sun.

Isono (214 Jericho Turnpike, Floral Park; 516-437-4552) and the more contemporary **Torigo** (196 Jericho Turnpike, Floral Park; 516-352-1116; www.torigorestaurant .com) are two good options in Floral Park for Japanese fare: sushi, tempura, bento boxes.

Fiore Italian Cuisine (142 Tulip Avenue, Floral Park; 516-775-8226; www.fiorerestaurant.com). Fiore satisfies the locals with Tuscan-inspired homemade specialties. Inventive main dishes include fettuccini with duck sautéed with a mushroom, spinach, dried cranberry, and garlic balsamic and oil base ($17), and fried banana cheesecake for dessert. Open Tues. through Sun. for dinner.

Koenig's (86 South Tyson Avenue, Floral Park; 516-354-2300; www.koenigsrestaurant .com). A Floral Park fixture since 1944. Relax and pull up a menu—it'll take a few lagers just to get through it. For old-school German fare, daily specials, and a generous selection of German wines and beers on tap. Adjacent to the Floral Park train station. Open daily for lunch and dinner.

Plattduetsche Park Restaurant (1132 Hempstead Turnpike, Franklin Square; 516-354-3131; www.parkrestaurant.com). Get your oompah on. Lederhosen optional Plattduetsche beer garden and restaurant has been celebrating Long Island's German heritage with traditional food, drink, and festivities since 1939. It's located a short drive from Belmont Park and Floral Park. Bar open daily; restaurant open Wed. through Sun. for lunch and dinner (and I'm totally serious about the lederhosen come festival time). Prost!

■ ■ ■ ■ **SPECIAL EVENTS**

The first Saturday that falls on or after June 5: **The Belmont Stakes** (www.belmontstakes.com).

Mid-July: Annual **Plattduetsche Volksfest** (www.parkrestaurant .com). The German heritage festival dates to 1884.

Late July: Annual **Thunderbird American Indian Mid-Summer Pow Wow** at the Queens County Farm Museum (www.queensfarm .org).

Mid-September: Annual **Antique Motorcycle Show** at the Queens County Farm Museum.

Mid-September: **Queens County Fair** at the Queens County Farm Museum.

■ ■ ■ ■ DRIVING TIP

A large dose of patience is required for entering, navigating, and leaving the Belmont Park parking lot come Belmont Stakes race day.

■ ■ ■ ■ STAY

Quality Inn (256-15 Jericho Turnpike, Floral Park; 718-343-9600; www.qualityinn.com). Online searches for hotels near Belmont Park bring up many JFK airport options (the addresses are listed as Jamaica—those are too far). This Quality Inn comes with a Nassau County address and a Queens County area code. It's on the Nassau/Queens border quite close to the racetrack and just across the street from many of the restaurants. Autumn rates start at $129.

■ ■ ■ ■ LIRR OPTION/ LOCAL TAXI INFO

Belmont Park enjoys its own LIRR train station with service from Jamaica station when racing is in session. From the track, a short cab ride gets you to Floral Park's restaurants. The restaurants are conveniently located within a five-minute walk from the Floral Park LIRR station (Hempstead branch). Two local cab services are AAA Taxi (516-328-8888) and Best Ford Taxi (516-327-8294).

■ ■ ■ ■ FYI

The official song of the Belmont Stakes is *New York, New York*.

The official libation for the Belmont Stakes is the Belmont Breeze. The recipe comes courtesy of www.belmontstakes.com. The ingredients are:

> 1½ oz. bourbon
> ¾ oz. Dry Sack sherry
> ¾ oz. fresh lemon juice
> ¾ oz. simple syrup
> 1½ oz. fresh orange juice
> 1½ oz. Ocean Spray cranberry juice

Shake all ingredients with ice and top with half 7 Up and half soda, approximately one ounce of each. Garnish with fresh strawberry, a mint sprig, and a lemon wedge.

▌▌▌▌ READS AND RESOURCES

Read *Tales from the Triple Crown* by Steve Haskin, a behind-the-scenes peek at the illustrious run for the Triple Crown.

▌▌▌▌ NEXT STOP

Queens County Farm Museum (73-50 Little Neck Parkway, Floral Park; 718-347-3276; www.queens farm.org). If the kids get intrigued by the horses at the racetrack, they'll love the barnyard critters that roam around the Queens Farm Museum. The history of the farm site dates to 1697, says the Web site. It is considered the longest continuously farmed land in the state and, at 47 acres, it's New York City's largest remaining tract of undisturbed farmland. A New York City entry in a book about Long Island? Yes. The telephone number says New York, but the address says Floral Park. It's actually on the Nassau/Queens border. The site includes historic barns and farm buildings, green-

Queens County Farm Museum

houses, an orchard and herb garden, and seasonal special events such as a corn maze every fall. But the real stars of this visit are the resident goats, hens, livestock, and rabbits among the two- and four-legged friends. Take Grand Central Parkway to exit 24 or Long Island Expressway to exit 32; proceed south along Little Neck Parkway.

15 • FOWL PLAY IN CENTRAL ISLIP: *The Long Island Ducks*

Central Islip, Hauppauge, Bay Shore, East Islip

If you build it, they really will come.

Move over New York Mets. No thank you, New York Yankees. Nassau and Suffolk's hometown field of dreams darlings are indeed the Long Island Ducks.

Members of the Atlantic League of Professional Baseball, the Long Island Ducks have been fulfilling local professional passion for America's favorite summer spectator pastime since 2000. Although the roster of players may not boast many household names, the management team certainly does. The Long Island Ducks co-ownership includes Major League Baseball luminaries Bud Harrelson, Frank Boulton, and current manager Gary Carter. Harrelson had a taste for the minor leagues after his storied MLB career and said it was time to bring some baseball to Long Island.

"We couldn't get a minor league team here because of the rules of Major League Baseball. This is Mets and Yankees territory," Harrelson said. "But independent baseball can be anywhere."

Harrelson explains that the Atlantic League of Professional Baseball was conceived in 1994. By 1998 six memberships (not franchises) already signed on. The Ducks membership got the green light and was founded the same year. With a little help from New York State to the tune of about $14 million for Suffolk County to build a new ballpark (the league requires its cities to build new stadiums), the Long Island Ducks made their inaugural season debut in 2000.

The ever-changing roster of talent ranges from minor leaguers on their way up the ranks as well as those recently released by the majors. Harrelson says that about 10 percent have played in the majors with the average age being about 28. In the minor league scheme of rankings, from the less-experienced A to about-to-make-it-to-the-big-leagues AAA-level, the Atlantic League of Professional Baseball ranks somewhere in the middle.

"This league is double-A caliber," Harrelson said. "Our players do move on to triple-A and even the big leagues."

Besides co-owning the team, Harrelson enjoys a number of on-site duties. He acts as first base coach. Well, sort of.

"I leave after the first inning," he said, "I then go to the skyboxes in uniform."

He offers a bit of a schmooze and some photo ops along the way. Harrelson doesn't go on the road, but he does attend every home game.

"I still sign autographs every day."

His favorite job of all, though, is batting practice.

"It's my exercise," he said. "It's my substitute for not being able to play. At 65, if I can still throw, and the guys root me on, I say great!"

Harrelson said he is most proud

of the fact of the type of entertainment the Ducks provide.

"I've been here on Long Island for 40 years and I know that there not many places to affordably entertain your kids," he said.

Harrelson says that in their 10-season history, individual ticket prices have only been raised $1. Tickets start at $10.

"So we're not Broadway. We're the movies. And that you can afford," Harrelson said. "Everyone has a great time."

They certainly do.

The very solid fan base that supports the Ducks is second to none. The Ducks play a complete minor league–style 140-game schedule: 70 games away and 70 games at Central Islip's Citibank Park. The Ducks own some bragging rights, too. Of the eight teams currently in the league, the Ducks hold the top annual attendance record. Their most recent

QuackerJack

Sagtikos Manor

2009 statistics saw some 400,000 fans in attendance for the season, again, the most for the league that year. That same year, the Ducks sold out 41 consecutive games in the 6,002-seat stadium.

The games combine expected big league sports thrills and endearing small town twists. Human hot dog races whip the crowd into a frenzy and local high school marching bands provide live entertainment. A spectator race pits two fans that place their forehead atop a baseball bat, spin around 10 times, and dizzily run in circles to the finish along the third base line. The prize: a year's supply of batteries. Seventh inning gets a proper *Take Me Out to the Ballgame* anthem and stretch, and on-field host Paul DeGrocco, clad in a bright orange sports blazer, keeps things briskly moving along.

And then there's QuackerJack. The Long Island Ducks resident mascot is adored by fans young and old. It seems that during the course of a game, QuackerJack poses for the camera, riles up the crowd, and pretty much meets and greets every section in that stadium.

Try to match that, major leagues.

▮▮▮▮ INFO

The Long Island Ducks play in the Liberty Division of the Atlantic League of Professional Baseball. The season runs late Apr. through late Sept.; into Oct. come playoffs time. Single-ticket prices $10–16. Call 631-940-3825 or visit www.li ducks.com.

▮▮▮▮ GETTING THERE

Citibank Park is at 3 Court House Drive, Central Islip. Access is off Carleton Avenue/County Road 17.

Check the Web site for complete directions. Parking is free.

The Bay Shore and Islip vicinity offers a number of worthy sight-seeing spots, public parks, and restaurants. Here's how to turn the destination into a full day's visit.

■■■■ OUTSIDE

Heckscher State Park (Take the Southern State Parkway to Heckscher Parkway in East Islip; 631-581-2100; www.nysparks.state.ny.us). Heckscher State Park offers Great South Bay scenery about 4 miles south of Citibank Park. The park was once home to the estate of William Nicoll, the founder of Islip. The park offers bay swimming, hiking, camping, playground and picnic areas, a swimming pool, and a boat launch. It's also home to a large population of white-tailed deer. Open year-round. $8 per carload or use your Empire Passport. Pool access costs $2 for adults (pool is closed Mon. and Tues.).

■■■■ SIGHTSEE

Sagtikos Manor (Montauk Highway at Manor Lane, West Bay Shore; 631-661-8348; www.sagtikosmanor.com). Original portions of stately Sagtikos Manor date to 1697. For a brief period, the estate was the headquarters of the British Army during the American Revolution. And yes, George Washington did sleep here during his 1790 tour of Long Island. The space abounds with period furnishings and authentic decor. Sagtikos Manor Historical Society offers summer tours led by costumed guides on Sun. in June, and Wed., Thurs., and Sun. in July and Aug. 1 PM—4 PM. Admission costs $7 for adults.

■■■■ WATERFRONT

Gardiner County Park (Montauk Highway and Manor Lane, West Bay Shore; 631-854-0935; www.co.suffolk.ny.us). On some days the dogs outnumber the people. Nothing to fear though, the pooches are all on leashes. Just across the street from Sagtikos Manor, the tranquil 230-acre Gardiner Park offers picnic areas, attracts area fisherman, and features a lovely tree-lined ¾-mile stroll from the entrance to the Great South Bay. It's quite a picturesque payoff with views of the Fire Island Lighthouse and the Robert Moses Causeway. Open daily. Admission is free.

■■■■ EAT

Pace's Steakhouse (325 Nesconset Highway, Hauppauge; 631-979-7676; www.pacessteakhouse.com). A good place for steaks and seafood before the baseball game. Aged steaks range from $29.95 (for the petite filet mignon) to $35.95 (for the 10-oz. size). Other entrées include rack of baby lamb ($29.95). Open daily for lunch and dinner.

Tula Kitchen (41 East Main Street/Montauk Highway, Bay Shore; 631-539-7183; www.tula kitchen.com). Warm and inviting with an inventive healthy menu to match. Sample Jackie's (for owner Jacqueline Sharlup) turkey loaf with root veggie pancakes, roasted carrots, and applesauce ($17). Mains $16–26. Open Tues., Wed., and weekends for dinner; Thurs. and Fri. for lunch and dinner.

Smokin' Al's Famous BBQ Joint (19 West Main Street/Montauk Highway, Bay Shore; 631-206-3000; www.smokinals.com). Top-notch fall-off-the-bone southern BBQ with all the trimmings. Generous portions and good prices. Full rack of Monster Beef Bones ($19.99) comes with two sides and choice of three sauces: original, sweet talkin', or rattlesnake. Open daily for lunch and dinner. Also in Massapequa Park (4847 Merrick Road; 516-799-4900).

Poppy's Luncheonette (499 Main Street/Montauk Highway, Islip; 631-581-2596). Crowd-pleasing basics: breakfast, burgers, salads, club rolls, grilled Philly sandwiches, and chicken or shrimp in a basket. Very reasonable prices and perfect for when you're taking the kids to the ballgame.

Fintans Irish Coffee Pub (131 Carleton Avenue, East Islip; 631-277-0007). Good Irish and pub fare in a casual setting. Velvety potato soup and spot-on shepherd's pie. Open daily for lunch and dinner.

▮▮▮▮ SHOP

The Long Island Ducks gift store at Citibank Park offers officially licensed L.I. Ducks memorabilia and apparel. The colors of choice: orange, green, and gray. Makes for a great Long Island souvenir. You can also order merchandise online.

▮▮▮▮ SPECIAL EVENTS

Summer: **Cultural Landscape Tours** held outdoors at Sagtikos Manor.

Early October: **Fall Festival** at Sagtikos Manor.

Mid-December: **Holiday Decorations** at Sagtikos Manor.

▮▮▮▮ DRIVING TIPS

The signs for the ballpark aren't so easy to spot. Be on the lookout for Court House Road off Carleton Avenue for Citibank Park parking.

Along the South Shore, a Main Street address often doubles as Montauk Highway/Route 27A.

■ ■ ■ ■ STAY

Sheraton Long Island Hotel (110 Vanderbilt Motor Pkwy., Hauppauge; 866-539-0036; www.starwoodhotels.com). About 4 miles from the ballpark. Rates start as low as $109 a night.

■ ■ ■ ■ LIRR OPTION/ LOCAL TAXI INFO

Citibank Park is accessible from the Central Islip LIRR train station (Ronkonkoma branch). Andre's Taxi (631-232-9696) provides service for about $7.

■ ■ ■ ■ FYI

The Long Island Ducks won the Atlantic League of Professional Baseball championship in 2004.

■ ■ ■ ■ READS AND RESOURCES

Visit the **Islip Chamber of Commerce** at www.islipchamberof commerce.com.

Visit the Chamber of Commerce of Greater Bay Shore at www.bay shorecommerce.com.

■ ■ ■ ■ NEXT STOP

For more family fun, start the day off at Splish Splash (see Chapter 17).

16 • TAKE A HIKE IN OAKDALE:
Connetquot River State Park and Preserve

Oakdale, Great River, Sayville, Patchogue, Shirley, Mastic Beach

Tell Gilbert Bergen to go take a hike and he'd probably A) do just that, and B) politely thank you.

Bergen, who says he's not one to a put on a suit or work in an office, seems to have found the dream job of a lifetime—he's been the park manager of the Connetquot River State Park and Preserve since 1960. Bergen says if you're looking to find a tranquil, calming walk in the woods, "the way the Long Island used to be," you're in luck at Connetquot.

Bergen explains that the park property, which hugs the Connetquot River, was first part of the William Nicoll grant of the town of Islip, which dates to 1683.

The geography of the area was strategic for a number of reasons. The river provided fishing and shipping opportunities—a mill was built in the 1700s, and Blue Point oysters, abundant in the nearby Great South Bay waters, were a tasty treat enjoyed all over the world. On land, the park's entrance road was the former Old South Country Road, the original main road from New York City to Montauk way back when.

Bergen says that in the early 1800s, "sportsmen discovered the place and came to hunt deer and fish." He adds that although the Southside Sportsman Club of Long Island was officially formed April 6, 1866, the on-site building headquarters dates to 1820. The building is now a registered Suffolk County landmark.

"The area was key to the development of the South Shore," Bergen said. "This was the original Gold Coast of Long Island."

Indeed, the North Shore didn't have dibs on the rich and famous of the day. A who's who of wealthy settlers included William K. Vanderbilt and financier and merchant William Bayard Cutting (see more info about him in the Bayard Cutting Arboretum entry). Incidentally, Bergen grew up on the Cutting estate—his father was a herdsman who tended jersey cattle on the estate grounds.

In 1963, the land was purchased by the state of New York.

"It opened as a public facility Aug. 20, 1973," Bergen said.

Today, the park encompasses 3,473 acres in all. Bergen says there are 50 miles of well-marked trails, including a portion of the Greenbelt Trail, as well as bridle paths. Bergen says the park is situated on glacial outwash plains.

"So it doesn't have a lot of hills," he said. "It's fairly level. It's perfect for bird-watchers and hikers."

In addition, the paths are wide enough as to avoid the dreaded deer tick so common in the area. Plenty of signage warns visitors of tick dos and don'ts.

Bergen says that as a park preserve, Connetquot is one of the few remaining parcels of Long Island that will never meet the wrath of developers.

"And I find it all very attractive," Bergen said. "I like this part of the world."

■■■■ INFO

Connetquot River State Park Preserve is open daily. Admission costs $6 per car load or use your Empire Passport. Call 631-581-1005 or visit www.nysparks.state.ny.us.

Guided walks highlight the gristmill, trout hatchery, preserve history, and a variety of ecological programs. The Catch and Release Fly Fishing Program costs $20 for a four-hour session.

■■■■ GETTING THERE

The Connetquot Park entrance is on the north side of Sunrise Highway, just west of Pond Road. You can only access the park traveling westbound off Sunrise Highway. So if you're coming from western Long Island, take the Southern State Parkway east to exit 44 (Sunrise Highway). Continue east along Route 27 Frontage Road/Oakdale Road. Turn left at Oakdale/Bohemia Road, cross over Sunrise Highway, then make a quick left again onto Sunrise Highway westbound and follow the signs.

Southside Sportsmen Club

Connetquot River Park

▮▮▮▮ SOUTH SHORE TOUR

After a hike in the Connetquot woods, here's a day trip worth exploring. This Great South Bay towns drive highlights some South Shore estates and a few iconic Main Streets. Tour stops include Great River, Oakdale, Sayville, Patchogue, Shirley, and Mastic Beach.

▮▮▮▮ GREAT RIVER

Bayard Cutting Arboretum (440 Montauk Highway, Great River; 631-581-1002; www.bayardcutting arboretum.com). This tranquil, refined respite was once the home of William Bayard Cutting, a financier and avid gardener who, along with his brother, started the sugar beet industry in the United States. His father, Robert Cutting, was the partner of steamship inventor Robert Fulton. The estate grounds highlight a variety of wildlife, dozens of bird species, and hundreds of plant species including an impressive array of spruce, fir, pine, yew, cypress, and hemlock—it's considered one of the most extensive conifer collections on Long Island. Lunch and Victorian tea is served at the on-site Hidden Oak Café in the former Cutting residence. Open year-round Tues. through Sunday. The $6 vehicle entrance fee is collected Apr. through Oct.

▮▮▮▮ OAKDALE

Idle Hour (150 Idle Hour Boulevard, Oakdale; 631-218-0784; www.dowling.edu). The original Idle Hour estate, built by William K. Vanderbilt, was destroyed by fire in 1899. (His son, William K. Vanderbilt II built the Vanderbilt estate in Centerport—see Chapter 5.) This second mansion, which overlooks the Connetquot River, cost $3 million to rebuild, a tidy sum today let alone for the turn of the last century. It's now home of Dowling College's Fortunoff Hall.

Mama's Pizza & Restaurant (1352 Montauk Highway, Oakdale; 631-567-0909). This informal eatery offers friendly service and excellent Italian fare and pizza.

▮▮▮▮ SAYVILLE

Long Island Maritime Museum (86 West Avenue, West Sayville; 631-447-8679; www.limaritime .org). Continue west along Montauk Highway and turn right when you see the sign. The Long Island Maritime Museum is home to *Modesty* and *Priscilla,* two tall ships that were refurbished onsite. The museum offers a Boatbuilders-in-Training program, which helps restore other heritage seafaring vessels. No experience? No problem. Just bring your nautical curiosity. Beautiful bay front scenery and park nearby as well.

Meadow Croft
Estate

Open daily. Admission costs $4 for adults.

Dozens of restaurants dot the Sayville culinary horizon. Start here and enjoy a Main Street stroll after your meal.

Sayville Aegean Café (35 Main Street, Sayville; 631-589-5529). Very good Greek fare in the heart of Sayville.

Café Joelle On Main Street (25 Main Street, Sayville; 631-589-4600; www.cafejoelle.net). Cozy, comfortable, and casual Café Joelle enjoys a loyal local clientele. And there's good reason. The ample menu offers everything from hearty burgers and pasta to inventive seafood, chicken, and even some authentic German specialties. Entrées from $8.95–27.95. Open daily for lunch and dinner; Sun. brunch.

Collins & Main (100 South Main Street, Sayville; 631-563-0805; www.collinsandmain.com). A dressier option for the area. Refined steak and seafood menu. Entrées from $24–36.

Sweet Mandarin (239 North Main Street; Sayville; 631-589-8822). This Asian bistro offers sushi and Japanese hibachi delicacies. Open daily for lunch and dinner.

Continue east along South Main Street/Middle Road, but don't drive too fast as a small sign and gravel road are the only clues to access the magnificently restored **Meadow Croft Estate** at San Souci Lakes Nature Preserve (Middle Road, Sayville; 631-567-1487). The manor is the former estate of John E. Roosevelt, a cousin of Theodore Roosevelt. The building dates to the 1890s. House tours are offered Sun. at 1 and 3 PM June through Oct.

The space is also home to what

may be Long Island's smallest winery, in **Loughlin Vineyards** (South Main Street, Sayville; 631-589-0027; www.loughlinvineyard .com), which encompasses a mere 6 acres. Tastings are held weekends from noon to 6 PM.

Land's End Motel (70 Brown's River Road, Sayville; 631-589-1888; www.landsendweddings .com) is half catering hall, half motel.

▪▪▪▪ PATCHOGUE

Make your way back to Montauk Highway and venture east to Patchogue. The first stop is the **Blue Point Brewery** (161 River Avenue, Patchogue; 631-475-6944; www.bluepointbrewing .com). Blue Point Brewery brews 12 varieties of original Long Island suds. The place is nothing to look at, but the beer sure is tasty. The tasting room is open Thurs. through Sat.

East Main Street offers a number of shops and dining as well as the centerpiece **Patchogue Theatre for the Performing Arts** (71 East Main Street, Patchogue; 631-207-1313; www.patchogue theatre.com). This busy theater, boasting 1,166 seats, helped revitalize the Main Street strip and offers first-rate year-round performances that include the likes of the Long Island Philharmonic, Broadway musical revivals, and

big name draws such as Judy Collins and Blue Öyster Cult.

PeraBell Food Bar (114 West Main Street, Patchogue; 631-447-7766; www.perabellfoodbar .com). Casual PeraBell offers a bistro/pub feel with a boisterous Sunday football crowd. The menu includes a generous selection of pub-style appetizers, soups, salads, and burgers, and an inventive variety of seafood and steak entrées ($16–28). Open daily for dinner, Sunday for lunch as well.

Gallo Tropical Restaurant (3 East Main Street, Patchogue; 631-475-4667). Columbian cuisine takes center stage at Gallo. Authentic starters include **Colombian chorizo sausage** served with griddle corn cake ($3.50). Entrées include the tropical quesadillas of steak, chicken, and shrimp ($12); a soup of the day—Saturdays feature oxtail or short rib soup served with rice and salad ($8.95); and native dishes such as the Tropical Platter of quarter rotisserie chicken, grilled steak, pork rind, fried egg, rice, beans, and plantain ($13.75). Seafood, sandwiches, and salads, too. Open daily.

Lawan Authentic Thai Restaurant (13 East Main Street, Patchogue; 631-687-1313; www .lawan.biz). The crispy boneless roast duck entrées ($15.95) are served in a number of ways with flavors that highlight tamarind, curry, or mixed herbs and spices. Dozens of other traditional Thai seafood and vegetarian dishes as well. Open weekdays for lunch; daily for dinner.

Mangia Mangia (69 East Main Street, Patchogue; 631-475-4774; www.mangiamangianow.com). For good Italian fare before your theater show. Open Tues. through Sun. for dinner.

Howard's Café (404 South Service Road, Patchogue; 631-758-6161). Make your way toward Sunrise Highway to find a burger paradise at Howard's Café. The gourmet burgers ($12) come in two dozen delectable ways.

■ ■ ■ ■ SHIRLEY

Smith Point County Park (L.I.E to exit 68 south on the William Floyd Parkway, Shirley; 631-244-7275; www.co.suffolk.ny.us). Located on the eastern end of Fire Island National Seashore, Smith Point features Atlantic Ocean beach swimming, surfing, fishing, camping, access to Otis Pike High Dune Wilderness Area, and hosts the TWA Flight 800 International Memorial. GreenKey county resident admission costs $5; tourist admission costs $10.

Smithpoint Beach Hut (William Floyd Parkway, Shirley; 631-281-7788; www.thebeachhuts .com). Grab a seafood snack at

this roadside shack after a day at the beach.

■ ■ ■ ■ MASTIC BEACH

William Floyd Estate (20 Washington Avenue, Mastic Beach; 631-399-2030; www.nps.gov). You've heard the name, but he's much more than a parkway and a school district. During the American Revolutionary War, Floyd acted as a major general of the Suffolk County militia. As a politician, he represented New York State at the first Continental Congress, was a U.S. congressman, and later a New York State senator. Perhaps his biggest claim to fame: he was a signer of the Declaration of Independence.

Eight generations of the Floyd family lived on the estate over the span of 250 years. The 600-plus-acre estate is now part of the Fire Island National Seashore and is run by the National Park Service, which often means well-documented history; painstaking care of the grounds and facilities; and a free or inexpensive visit. Free guided one-hour tours of the 25-room Old Mastic House are offered every half-hour during opening hours.

The grounds are open 9 AM – 5 PM Fri. through Sun. and holiday Mondays from Memorial Day through mid-Nov. Don't forget the insect repellent come high summer season.

■■■■ TIPS ON TICKS

Ticks prefer grasses that range in height from about 6 to 18 inches. Stick to the main trails.

Wear insect repellent. Equally, get your dog a tick collar if bringing the pooch along for the hike.

Wear long sleeves and tuck your pant legs inside your socks. Same goes for shirttails, too. Hey, you're on a hike—it's not a fashion show.

Check yourself after the hike (enjoy this task with a loved one).

If you find a tick attached to your body, use tweezers to wriggle the tick free in the same direction the tick is attached.

Discard the tick down the toilet and apply antiseptic to the bite.

Call a doctor if you develop a fever, rash, or severe headaches.

Take William Floyd Parkway, Route 46, south to Havenwood Drive. Turn left onto Havenwood Drive, which turns into Neighborhood Road. Continue 2 miles east to and turn left onto Park Drive. Follow the signs.

■■■■ LIRR OPTION/ LOCAL TAXI INFO

Connetquot Park is accessible from the Oakdale LIRR train station (Montauk branch). Colonial Taxi (631-589-3500) provides area service for about $12.

■■■■ FYI

The Paumanok Path—now that's a hike! This hiking trail stretches some 110 miles beginning in Rocky Point and ending in Montauk Point State Park.

Anytime you see State Park in an attraction's name, you can use your Empire Passport.

■■■■ READS AND RESOURCES

For information about the **Long Island Greenbelt**, visit Long Island Greenbelt Trail Conference at www.ligreenbelt.org or call 631-360-0753.

Friends of Connetquot also host their own walking and bird-watching tours throughout the year at Connetquot State Park. Visit www.friendsofconnetquot .org.

Visit **Sayville** at www.sayville .com.

Visit **Patchogue Village** at www.patchoguevillage.org.

■ ■ ■ ■ NEXT STOP

For more great outdoors hiking Long Island-style, visit the **Pine Barrens Trail Information Center** (County Road III, L.I.E exit 70 north, one-quarter mile north on your right in Manorville; seasonal phone 631-852-3449; www.pb .state.ny.us and www.suffolk countyny.gov). The visitor center offers access to hiking trails as well as environmental education info. Open Fri. through Mon. from May through Oct.

The William Floyd Estate visit is also a good way to start a west-to-east tour of the Moriches, Westhampton, and the Big Duck (see Chapter 21).

17 • WET AND WILD IN RIVERHEAD: *Splish Splash*

Riverhead, Calverton, Wading River, Manorville

Nothing makes Chip Cleary happier than the thrill of a good amusement park ride. Adding a little water to the mix makes the experience even better.

Cleary clearly knows a thing or two about amusement park rides. He started his career at another Long Island fun spot, Adventureland Amusement Park in Farmingdale. In 1991, he and his partners founded Splish Splash, Long Island's premier water park. Today, Cleary acts as senior vice president for Palace Entertainment, the current Splish Splash owner, and also oversees a dozen other water parks across the country. So what makes for a good water park ride?

"First you need a story," Cleary said. Cleary describes water parks when he first started in the amusement park industry in the 1980s as "rides in the middle of a farm field." He wondered how long those rides would stay popular.

"If you stand in line for a great ride your mind builds up with anticipation," Cleary said. "So

our premise from the beginning was that every ride needs to have a story."

Take Alien Invasion, for example. At first glimpse you've got a really long tunnel and great big green funnel. Not so, says Cleary. There's more to the ride than that. The way Cleary describes it, a spaceship has crashed into the earth and has taken over the water park. At the ride's entrance, scattered debris and a crashed spaceship sit near the pump house, spurting water everywhere. The visitor is, in turn, captured, minimized for transport, and shipped off to a distant planet via a big green 70-foot funnel, also known as the communication portal to the alien's home.

I like his version better.

"As goofy or campy as it sounds, people really get into it," Cleary said. "It's no longer the big green funnel slide. It becomes Alien Invasion."

Cleary's amusement park logic is simple: You're going to have some lines; you might as well offer some entertainment along the way.

"It tends to make the line experience a little better, a little quicker," he said.

Next: You've got to have a great ride. Cleary says that the water park industry is fairly new to the amusement park scene—the industry debuted in the 1980s—but folks have now had the chance to enjoy water parks for some three decades. Visitors know what to expect and want the envelope pushed.

"So you have to have something more than grab a tube, climb up a hill, and go down a slide."

Or, if you do have the slide ride formula, take it one step further. Cases in point are two current park favorites: the new Dr. Von Dark, a water slide ride that takes place completely in the dark, and the gravity-defying Cliff Diver, which lets thrill seekers swoop down an 80-foot slide, 50 feet of which are in complete freefall.

"That's the one ride where there's a chicken-out factor, "Cleary said. "Folks climb that tower, and that's a loooooong climb. They sometimes change their minds."

The top of the platform, which is above the tree line, offers a pretty spectacular view of the Peconic River area.

"But there is a percentage of riders that say, 'nice view,' turn around, and head back down the stairs."

That said, Cleary adds the ride is perfectly safe. He knows. He's been on it. In fact, Cleary has personally enjoyed every ride in his park.

"And I plan on going on every ride in the universe," he said. "I'm a ride person. I like rides. I love to experience them. And if you do what I do, to enjoy a good guest experience, you have to try them out."

Cleary says the demographic who visits Splish Splash range from young thrill seekers to families out enjoying the day.

Riverhead attractions

"We try to balance it," he said. "There's something for everyone, from Cliff Diver to simpler inner tube rides such as the Lazy River, a spa pool, and the wave pool. We want grandma and grandpa here, too."

Cleary also offers a number water park tips. Although the space abounds with many shade trees—a most welcome attribute on the hottest of summer days, sunscreen is a must. In addition, don't wear your best bathing suit.

"In the early days of water parks, people wore bathing suits that were a little more show biz and a little less structural," Cleary said. "Over the years, America has discovered that coming to a water park isn't a fashion show."

So wear a comfortable—but sturdy—bathing suit. Also, don't bring your best towels. An old one will do just fine.

"You and a thousand of your friends are visiting on the same day," Cleary said. "The towels begin to look alike."

Finally, get there early and don't go with the flow.

"First in gets best pick of rides," Cleary said.

He adds that many amusement parks are designed in a circular layout.

"Naturally, right handers tend to start on their right. Try going left and work against the crowd."

Cleary says the last element essential for a water park is water. But think much more than the traditional swimming pool.

"I'm a big believer that fountains, geysers, misters, bubblers, and blasters go a long way," Cleary said. "Why not celebrate water? It's the reason why you're here, after all."

■■■■ INFO

Splish Splash is open weekends Memorial Day through the first day of summer and then daily through Labor Day. Admission costs $36.99 for general admission and $27.99 for children less than 48" tall and seniors. Call 631-727-3600 or visit www.splish splashlongisland.com.

■■■■ GETTING THERE

Splish Splash is at 2549 Splish Splash Drive in Riverhead. Take the L.I.E. eastbound to exit 72 west. Take the west ramp and turn left at the first traffic light onto Splish Splash Drive.

■■■■ WATERFRONT

Atlantis Marine World (431 East Main Street, Riverhead; 631-208-9200; www.atlantismarineworld .com). In keeping with the area's water theme, Atlantis Marine

World, Long Island's premier aquarium, has become one of the more popular attractions along Riverhead's Main Street. The space features resident jellyfish, electric eels, and sand sharks. Exhibitions include a touch tank and a shipwreck artificial reef. Daring adventurers can go on a real shark dive ($140). Not-so-daring landlubbers can simply kiss a sea lion. Open year-round. Admission costs $21.50 for adults; $18.50 for children.

Peconic Paddler (89 Peconic Avenue, Riverhead; 631-727-9895; www.peconicpaddler.com). At 15 miles long, the lazy, tranquil Peconic River is Long Island's longest. Most of it lies within the boundaries of the Long Island Pine Barrens. Peconic Paddler offers up-close views with sea kayak, canoe, and stand-up paddleboard sales and rentals.

■■■■ SIGHTSEE

Hallockville Museum Farm (6038 Sound Avenue, Riverhead; 631-298-5292; www.hallockville.com). Listed on the National Register of Historic Places, this 28-acre farm preserve pays homage to Long Island's agricultural past through docent-led guided tours of 18 historic buildings that date to the mid-18th century. Admission costs $7 for adults. Open Fri. through Sun. 11 AM–4 PM.

■■■■ OUTSIDE

Long Island Game Farm (638 Chapman Boulevard; Manorville; 631-878-6644; www.longisland gamefarm.com). A Long Island institution since 1970. The 25-acre Long Island Game Farm offers a petting zoo and a crowd of critters large and small from camels to kangaroos, giraffes to kinkajous. Open daily Apr. through Oct. Admission costs about $17.50 for adults; $15.50 for children.

■■■■ EAT RIVERHEAD

Funcho's Fajita Grill (1156 West Main Street, Riverhead; 631-369-7277; www.funchosfajitagrill .com). Funcho's is fantastic. This roadside-style eatery offers fresh fresh fresh Tex-Mex fare, hearty portions, great value, and authentic Mexican beers. It's quite popular with the locals for take-out orders. It's a tight squeeze inside, but there are picnic tables outside during warmer weather. Also in Westhampton Beach (127 Main Street; 631-288-2408).

Snow Flake Ice Cream Shop (1148 West Main Street/Route 25, Riverhead; 631-727-4394; www .snowflakeicecream.com). Adjacent to Funcho's, save some room for some sweet treats from Snow Flake, such as pumpkin ice cream in season.

Tweed's Restaurant & Buffalo Bar (17 East Main Street, Riverhead; 631-208-3151; www.tweeds restaurant.com). A more upscale option in downtown Riverhead for seafood, steaks, wildfowl, and game meats. Entrées range from $19 for the Tweed's bison burger to $36 for grilled bison cowboy steak. A lovely selection of Long Island wines, too. Open for lunch, dinner, and weekend brunch.

Athens Gyro and Grill (33 East Main Street, Riverhead; 631-727-1301; www.athensgyro.com). This downtown eatery offers excellent Greek fare, an ample menu, and good value. Entrées $13–21. Open Mon. through Sat. for lunch and dinner.

Digger O'dell's (58 West Main Street, Riverhead; 631-369-3200; www.diggerspub.net). For tasty pub fare in a casual relaxed atmosphere. Digger O'dell's gets extra points for offering an online coupon for a free pint of Guinness. The menu offers a slew of starters and bar snacks, burgers and sandwiches, and steaks and Irish specialties such as the Tipperary chicken pot pie ($15.99).

Spicy's Barbecue (225 West Main Street, Riverhead; 631-727-2781). Spot-on BBQ at some of the best prices on Long Island. The unique chopped beet and pork BBQ sandwich tallies in at only $4.39. Add a large macaroni salad side for an extra $3.89. You can even buy the fall-off-the-bone ribs one piece at a time for $1.89 each. Open daily for lunch and dinner.

Peconic River Herb Farm (2749 River Road, Calverton; 631-369-0058; www.prherbfarm.com). This 14-acre riverfront seasonal nursery, open mid-Apr. through mid-Oct., retails a variety of herb and specialty plants.

■■■■ SHOP

Tangers Outlet (1770 West Main Street, Riverhead; 631-369-2732; www.tangeroutlet.com). Tangers boasts 165 specialty outlet stores including apparel designers Kenneth Cole, Anne Klein, Banana Republic, Hugo Boss, and Tommy Hilfiger, as well as the likes of Williams-Sonoma, Restoration Hardware, and Pottery Barn. Don't let the Main Street address fool you; this is mall-style shopping.

■■■■ SPECIAL EVENTS

Early October: Wildwood State Park annual **Fall Festival** (www.nysparks.state.ny.us).

■■■■ AFTER DARK

Atlantis Marine World hosts an annual Aquarium Sleepover, often the Friday after Thanksgiving 6 PM–7 AM the next morning.

The adventure includes story-telling, a movie, animal encounters, dinner, and breakfast. BYOSB—bring your own sleeping bag. About $40 for members; $60 for nonmembers. Reservations required at 631-208-9200, ext. 426.

■■■■ STAY

Hilton Garden Inn (2038 Old Country Road, Riverhead; 631-727-2733; www.hiltongardeninn.hilton.com) is a five-minute drive from Splish Splash. Rates start at about $199 a night. Hotel stays/Splish Splash packages are available.

Wildwood State Park (Hulse Landing Road, Wading River; 631-929-4314; www.nysparks.state.ny.us). Rough it! Located directly on the Long Island Sound about a 10-minute drive from Riverhead, the 600-acre Wildwood Sate Park offers beach access, hiking, and a campground with tent and trailer sites. Open Apr. though Columbus Day weekend. Park access costs about $8 or use your Empire Passport. Camping sites cost $15 a night.

■■■■ DRIVING TIPS

Riverhead Raceway (Route 58, Riverhead, L.I.E. exit 73; 631-727-0010; www.riverheadraceway.com). Brings new meaning to

cash for clunkers. Riverhead Raceway has been thrilling car racing fans with Figure 8 stock car, monster truck, and even school bus races since 1951. You can enter your car in any number of annual drag races and demolition derbies for a top prize of about $400.

■■■■ LIRR OPTION/ LOCAL TAXI INFO

Splish Splash is accessible from the Riverhead station (Ronkonkoma branch). Riverhead Taxi (631-369-9200) provides local service. About $10 to Splish Splash for one person.

■■■■ FYI

The Travel Channel ranked Splish Splash the fifth best water park in the country.

■■■■ READS AND RESOURCES

Visit the **Riverhead Chamber of Commerce** at www.riverheadchamber.com.

■■■■ NEXT STOP

The stars come out at night at the Vanderbilt Planetarium (see chapter 5).

UNIQUE—
LONG ISLAND—
NEW YORK

18 • REAL CORKERS ALONG THE NORTH FORK: *A Vineyards Tour*

Aquebogue, Jamesport, Mattituck, Cutchogue, Peconic, Southold

Cheers! to Long Island's bustling wine industry. A North Fork winery tour on any given day offers some good taste, and you'll meet some real corkers along the way.

Charles Massoud, owner of Paumanok Vineyards, moved to the North Fork in 1983. His was one of the first of a dozen vineyards to establish themselves in the area. Only four of those originals remain, but today some 45 wine producers, 25 of which are full-service estates, call Long Island home.

What was the attraction to owning a vineyard?

"Well I always liked to drink good wine," the affable, soft-spoken Massoud said.

"I grew up in a family where my parents always drank wine with their meals. As children, we could taste."

Massoud grew up in Lebanon and attended Christian school. He went to mass every day. The Tuesday service offered the Greek Catholic rite.

"They would give people bread and wine in communion," Massoud said. "And I made sure I went to communion every Tuesday. So early on, I developed a taste for wine."

After university, Massoud got a job with IBM in 1970. He soon transferred to Kuwait with his wife, Ursula.

"It was a different culture for many reasons," he said. "We got there to find out they had prohibition. It was problematic to buy beer and wine, but you could buy scotch on the black market."

Massoud asked his coworkers what they did if they wanted a drink.

"They said, 'you have to make your own.'"

So he did. He had two options: beer or wine. Massoud says it was rather easy to get a beer- or wine-making kit through customs (officials were more concerned with the end product). He found beer "a pain" to make, so he gave winemaking a try. He's been doing it ever since.

"The wine, surprisingly, was quite good," he said.

Massoud hosted informal private wine-tasting parties with friends and coworkers and took lots of notes. He also had a little help from his in-laws: Ursula comes from a winemaking family in Germany.

"Little by little that hobby of necessity found a nurturing ground."

The lightbulb now lit, Massoud and his wife entertained the notion of owning a vineyard in their retirement years. They originally thought they would buy in Germany. When Massoud and his family left Kuwait, he transferred to the New York metropolitan area. One year later during a rainy afternoon sitting in front of the fireplace in his Connecticut

North Fork sights

home, Massoud, with a glass of cabernet sauvignon in hand, stumbled upon a *New York Times* article about Long Island vineyards. That really caught his attention.

"They're making wine right in our backyard," he told Ursula.

Three months later, the pair spent an afternoon at the Hargrave Vineyards (now Castello di Borghese), the first Long Island winery, and returned home all excited about his own future winemaking prospects.

"Over the next three years we planned, studied, absorbed, met with winemakers, and learned everything we could," Massoud said. "Long Island presented a great opportunity to produce a high-quality wine. So we decided to make the leap."

Massoud placed a few offers on some farms.

"If it didn't work, at least we'd still have a nice property not far from the beach." he said.

But it did work.

In 1983 Massoud planted 10 acres. Today he cultivates 72 acres of farmland devoted to eight varieties of wine, four red and four white. Incidentally, his son is now the head winemaker. Paumanok Vineyards produces 8,000 to 9,000 cases of wine a year.

"But we think of yield in terms

of high quality. That's our philosophy."

Massoud's "retirement" has never tasted sweeter.

■■■■ GETTING THERE

Take the L.I.E. to the last exit, exit 73. The exit ramp leads to County Road 58, eastbound, which turns into Route 25. Route 25 continues to the end of the North Fork.

The larger vineyard tasting rooms are open daily throughout the year, except for certain holidays. Reservations are often required for bridal showers, limos, and tour buses.

The Long Island Wine Council, at www.liwines.com, is a great resource to help you select a few full-service vineyards that offer tasting rooms. That said, you can pretty much hop in the car and just drive along Route 25 and create your own impromptu vineyards tour. It's fun to compare the wines and tasting rooms while people-watching.

After a visit to the more refined Paumanok Vineyards during a busy summer Saturday, venture farther east to Bedell Cellars Vineyards. The tasting room offers an indoor bar, an outdoor terrace, sexy bottle label art, a mod decor in a renovated potato barn, and does a brisk Saturday-afternoon wine-tasting business. Folks arrived in stretch limos, usually

bridal shower parties, and even by bicycle.

Farther east still, the Lenz Winery tasting room employed a more casual feel—a *Cheers*-style where-everybody-knows-your-name sentiment established itself firmly in the first few minutes.

"This business is more family than competitive," said Lenz tasting room manager Barbara Reuschle. She adds many employees in the small but well-established North Fork wine industry—whether you're a winemaker or tasting room wine pourer—know each other quite well.

"We all enjoy each other's company," Reuschle said

And that's some pretty tasty company to keep.

■■■■ INFO

Paumanok Vineyards is at 1074 Main Road/Route 25 in Aquebogue. Call 631-722-8800 or visit www.paumanok.com.

Bedell Cellars Vineyards is at 36225 Main Road/Route 25 in Cutchogue. Call 631-734-7537 or visit www.bedellcellars.com.

The Lenz Winery is at Route 25/Main Road in Peconic. Call 631-734-6010 or visit www.lenz wine.com.

The Tasting Room showcases a number of the smaller boutique vineyards that don't necessarily have their own tasting rooms per se. The vineyards highlighted at the Tasting Room include Bouké Wines and Sherwood House Vineyards of Mattituck, Bridge Vineyards of Cutchogue, Christiano Family Vineyards and Sparkling Pointe of Southold, Comtesse Thérèse of Aquebogue, Medolla Vineyards and Onabay Vineyards of Peconic, and Schneider Vineyards of Riverhead. The Tasting Room is housed in a former speakeasy at 2885 Peconic Lane in Peconic. Hours are Fri. to Sun. 11 AM–6 PM. Call 631-765-6404 or visit www.tastingroomli.com.

■ ■ ■ ■ WINE CAMP

Summer camp never tasted so good. **Wine Camp** is a midweek four-day interactive adventure for adults only that lets foodies participate in wine tastings, gourmet meals, vineyard tours, meetings with winemakers, behind-the-scenes peeks at the winery, and lessons about food and wine pairings. All levels of wine connoisseurs are welcome. Just bring your curiosity.

Wine Camp costs about $899 a person. Meals, lodging, and transportation around the North Fork are included. Wine Camp is held four to six times a year. For more information and upcoming dates call 631-495-9744 or visit www.winecamp.org.

■ ■ ■ ■ OUTSIDE

Laurel Lake Preserve (Entrance along Route 25, Southold; 631-765-1800; www.southoldtown.northfork.net). Suffolk County's Town of Southold—pretty much all of the North Fork—oversees six East End preserves including its largest, Laurel Lake, a 400-acre property dense with a hardwood forest, abundant local fauna, and a 30-acre body of water called a kettle hole lake for which the preserve is named. A well-marked hiking trail runs to the water's edge and throughout the preserve.

■ ■ ■ ■ SIGHTSEE

Cutchogue Village Green (Route 25 and Case's Lane, Cutchogue). It's a quick visit, but it's hard to pass up this irresistible slice of local history. Run by the Cutchogue—New Suffolk Historical Council, the Cutchogue Village Green grouping of historical houses and landmarks dates to 1649. The historical buildings on-site include the Old House, a farmhouse, schoolhouse, and carriage house, which now serves as a small gift store.

■ ■ ■ ■ WATERFRONT

Eagle's Neck Paddling Company (49295 Main Road, Southold; 631-765-3502; www.eaglesneck.com).

Up the creek; paddle included. Offers daily and weekly canoe and kayak rentals, as well as guided tours of local waterways including Arshamomaque Pond and Gooseneck Creek.

■ ■ ■ ■ EAT

Modern Snack Bar (628 Main Road/Route 25, Aquebogue; 631-722-3655; www.modernsnackbar .com). A seasonal spot for spot-on comfort food. From tuna melts and hot turkey sandwiches ($8.95 each) for lunch to chicken croquettes and meat loaf ($12.85 each) for dinner. Seafood, salads, and burgers, too. Open Tues. through Sun. for lunch and dinner Apr. through mid-Dec.

Love Lane Kitchen (240 Love Lane, Mattituck; 631-298-8989; www.lovelanekitchen.com). Quaint, cozy, and casual Love Lane Kitchen serves quality bistro fare from sunup to sundown. Rancheros omelets ($9) for breakfast; Cuban pork sandwiches ($12) for lunch; and dinner entrées that range from burgers ($12) to Long Island duck tagine ($26). Open Mon. and Tues. for breakfast, lunch, and very early dinner; open Wed. through Sun. for breakfast, lunch, and dinner.

A Mano Osteria & Wine Bar (13550 Main Road/Route 25, Mattituck; 631-298-4800; www.amano restaurant.com). Home is where the hearth is. Comfy digs that feature a centerpiece wood brick oven where delectable pizza pie ($15) in a variety of flavors is created. The prix fixe menu ($24.95) offers an abundance of homemade Italian specialties. Outdoor patio. Local Long Island wines. Open daily for dinner; weekends for lunch.

The North Fork Table and Inn (57225 Route 25, Southold; 631-765-0177; www.northforktable andinn.com). Seasonal and local ingredients and wines play a big role in the simple and fine serendipitous contemporary American fare served up at the table portion of North Fork Table and Inn. If you're day-tripping the local vineyards and are in the mood for a culinary treat, the tasting menu (about $85) will reaffirm all that is gastronomically good about Long Island. Of note: roasted baby beets, Long Island braised duck ravioli, and coconut tapioca. Light, airy dining room. Open weekends for lunch; daily for dinner. Room rates about $275–300.

Braun's Seafood 2 Go (30840 Main Road/Route 25, Cutchogue; 631-734-6700; www.braunsea food.com). The locals buy all their seafood fresh at Braun Seafood Company fish market. The adjacent seafood takeout store enjoys a brisk business with summer staples such as chowders, fried cherrystone clams, lobster rolls, and sushi. Grab a snack to go for a wine taste just next door at **Peconic Bay Winery** (31320 Main Road; 631-734-7361; www.peconicbaywinery.com). Proceed with patience, courtesy, and a friendly wave in the busy parking lot.

■■■■ FARM STANDS

Bring home some delicious North Fork bounty with you available at three fine East End farmstands.

Briermere Farms (4414 Sound Avenue, Riverhead; 631-722-3931; www.briemere.com). The address is Riverhead, but this part of town is more North Fork farm country than Main Street. If you're in the area for food and wine, you might as well bring home some home baked pies while you're at it. And Briermere offers the best pies in all the land.

Garden of Eve Farm (4558 Sound Avenue, Riverhead at the intersection of Sound Avenue and Route 83/Northville Turnpike; 631-523-6608; www.gardenofeve farm.com) offers a full line of organic products and produce as well as a garlic lover's delight—join them in late Sept. for their annual Garlic Festival.

Sang Lee Farms (25180 County Road 48, Peconic; 631-734-7001; www.sangleefarms.com) special-izes in heirloom tomatoes, and Asian, mesclun, and baby greens. Their online store also offers dressings, jellies, pestos, and soups. Farm stand hours are daily during the summer season.

■■■■ SHOP

Jamesport Country Store (Main Road/Route 25, Jamesport; 631-722-8048). Americana and outdoorsy antiques with an exterior front lot that doubles as a picturesque East End photo op.

Ellmers Handmade Amish Furniture (Route 25, Cutchogue; 631-734-2723).

Ellmers roadside furniture store is fun to browse inside and out.

■■■■ SPECIAL EVENTS

Mid-June: **Mattituck Strawberry Festival** (1175 Route 48, Mattituck; www.mattituckstrawberry festival.org). A North Fork staple since 1954. The fair-style flair includes arts and crafts, amusement rides, and fireworks, as well as the crowning of the Strawberry Queen. Festival food includes fried chicken, funnel cakes, and, of course, strawberry shortcake for everyone. Weekend adult admission costs $5; rides extra. It's sponsored by the local Lions Club, so all proceeds go to local North Fork charities.

Early August: **Old Town Art and Crafts Guild Arts and Crafts**

Jedediah Hawkins Inn

Show. On the Cutchogue Village Green. Visit www.oldtownguild .com.

▌▌▌▌ AFTER DARK

Mattituck 8 Cinemas (10095 Main Road/Route 25, Mattituck; 631-298-7469). First-run flicks; eight screens in all.

▌▌▌▌ DRIVING TIPS

Be prepared for busy stop-and-go weekend summer and fall traffic along two-lane Route 25.

▌▌▌▌ STAY

Jedediah Hawkins Inn & Restaurant (400 Jamesport Avenue, Jamesport; 631-722-2900; www .jedediahhawkinsinn.com). The 1800s-era Victorian Jedediah Hawkins Inn was restored by local builder Jeff Hallock and Long Island oncologist Dr. Frank Arena. After a painstaking three-year restoration project, the space opened as a B&B and restaurant in 2005. The six-room designer showcase—each room was created by a different interior designer—ranges from the nautical-themed Indigo Room ($250 a night, weekdays) to the roomy Belvedere Suite ($600 a night during weekdays). If the prices are out of your budget, it's still worth a drive past and a peek inside. Check out the main floor restaurant bathroom, which resembles a fun faux beach-side cabana.

▌▌▌▌ LIRR OPTION/ LOCAL TAXI INFO

The North Fork is accessible from the Mattituck and Southold LIRR stations (Ronkonkoma branch). Island Cab Company (631-765-8622) offers area service.

The LIRR offers a number of Long Island one-day getaway packages, which include train

fare and coach bus accommodations. A **LIRR Long Island Wine
County Tour** is offered four times
a year July through Sept. The
price is about $45. Visit www.mta
.info. Click LIRR, Travel, Getaways
and Packages.

Off the Vine Tours offers custom private North Fork wine
country tours from birthdays to
bachelorette parties. The best
part of all: you can sample delicious wines and leave the driving
to someone else. Call 631-779-
3278 or visit www.offthevinetours
.com.

▮▮▮▮ FYI

Need some simple guidelines on
how to properly taste wine? Use
all of your senses and keep these
tips in mind:

Appearance: Check a wine's
color as well as its clarity.

Swirl: Gently swirl the wine in
your glass. This will aerate the
wine and release its natural aro-
mas.

Smell: The nose knows—get
your sniffer into that glass.

Taste: No big gulp, but a generous sip. Let it linger on your
palate and tongue.

Savor: How did it taste. Did you
like it? It's okay to take notes.
Cheers!

▮▮▮▮ READS AND RESOURCES

Read: Long Island Wine Country:
Award-Winning Vineyards of the
North Fork and the Hamptons by
Jane Taylor and Bruce Curtis.

▮▮▮▮ NEXT STOP

Finish your North Fork tour in
Greenport (see Chapter 8).

19 • CAST OF (HISTORICAL) CHARACTERS IN OLD BETHPAGE: *Old Bethpage Village Restoration*

Bethpage, Farmingdale, Massapequa, Babylon

Old Bethpage Village Restoration accurately re-creates 19th-century Long Island life through 16 historical buildings that date from pre-Revolutionary times to 1866. The main buildings on-site all come from previous Long Island locations except for the Powell Farmhouse, which stands on its original home. The historical buildings are something to see, and the characters that bring the place to life are, well, something else.

The first stop is the Layton General store. Dating to 1866, it's one of the youngest buildings on the premises. It originally stood in East Norwich, 9 miles to the north at the intersection of Northern Boulevard and Route 106.

"It was a little department store of its day," said volunteer Bob Mesard. The place sold everything from groceries such as coffee, tea, sugar, and rice to kitchen wares and bolts of cloth—everything the Long Island farmer needed. A number of period artifacts are on display.

Mesard says that except for except for kitchen and roof, the building was shipped practically intact. On one side was the general store; on the other side was the Layton family residence. Visitors can take a stroll about the house, which contains two upstairs bedrooms, a living room with pull-out sofa and pump organ that still works, and a kitchen with sink pump that indicates indoor plumbing—it's the only building on the site that boasts that amenity.

"They were fairly well off," Mesard said. "The family originally owned a hotel in East Norwich. And business was pretty good."

Mesard doesn't portray Layton per se, but he is dressed in time-appropriate clothing. However, come the annual 1880s Memorial Day/Decoration Day festivities, he does take on the role of the local Methodist minister.

"I do a nice invocation and benediction," Mesard said.

"Someone else does the fire and brimstone."

Down the road a way at the circa-1810 Ritch House and Shop, we meet hatmaker Ken Quinn. Quinn started as a volunteer in 1990 and went on staff a few years later. How did he get his start making hats?

"They told me to," says Quinn deadpan. "One day someone left, I filled in, and here I am."

In the past two decades Quinn has become a pretty good hat-maker. Each hat typically takes four to eight hours of working time and a bit longer for the drying process. All of his hats are authentic reproductions and all are for sale. The most popular wide-brimmed farmer-style retails for $65 (that's today's prices).

The next stop is the Powell Farmhouse, which is restored to 1855. It's where we meet the very affable Marty Jancheson, a staff member for almost three decades. His is a typical day at a Long Island farm. And that means lots of old-fashioned chores such as feeding the animals, cleaning the stalls, and some new tasks as well, including greeting hundreds of schoolchildren every day. The barnyard critters on hand include oxen, cows, chicken, pigs, sheep, and ducks—an orchestra of animals that boister-ously moo, cluck, oink, baa, and quack in unison.

And Jancheson calls most of the animals by name.

"You've got to talk to them," he said. "They have their own personalities."

For example, a resident cow occasionally takes a stroll when Jancheson forgets to tie down the gate.

"But she knows when it's time for dinner and always returns," he said. "They have very good internal clocks."

The next stop means it's time

A friendly face at Old Bethpage Village

Old Bethpage Village Layton Store

for a libation at the 1850s-era Noon Inn. But inn and barkeep Fred Fischer, a volunteer for 25 years, serves up only nonalcoholic beverages.

"We're purely abstentious in the true Methodist way," Fischer said. "Our provender here is root beer, birch beer, and ginger ale."

Fischer explains that the local temperance society was a way to combat the nearby Hempstead militia's heavy drinking problem. He has the backstory down pat.

"I've also found the 18th century riveting," Fischer said.

He adds that if a bar or inn served alcohol, the drinking age was 14 back then, the space also needed to provide food and a place to sleep.

"And lodging meant bed space," Fischer said. "Not a room. Not a bed. Bed space."

At a cost of about 25 cents a night, when the daily wage was about $1 to $1.25 a day, "it wasn't a bad deal by today's standards."

Finally, we meet on-site schoolmarm Kathleen Gillen, a staff member for four years—a newcomer in these parts. Her one-room schoolhouse, which was built in 1823 and restored to 1845, originally stood in Manhasset. Most of the contents, except the desks, are real, from the book straps to the vintage Long Island map and the poster of all 11 United States presidents of the time. In 1845, James Polk held the seat. I mistakenly ask Gillen if she dresses in her costume before she arrives for work.

"What's wrong with this? This is not a costume," she says pokerfaced. Her coworkers' quick wit and savvy has already rubbed off quite well.

A history major, she graduated in 2009 with aspirations of

Old Bethpage Village Restoration

becoming a lawyer, says she has pumped gas and occasionally run in the local convenience store for a loaf of bread dressed as is in her long gray dowdy dress. She's gotten her share of stares in public.

"I just play along," she said. "For now this is a dream job. It's just a lot of fun."

▪▪▪▪ INFO

Old Bethpage Village Restoration is open from early Apr. through Nov. Peak season hours are 10 AM–5 PM Wed. through Sun. Admission costs about $10 for adults and $7 for children and seniors. Call 516-572-8400 or visit www.nassaucountyny.gov.

▪▪▪▪ GETTING THERE

Old Bethpage Village is at 1303 Round Swamp Road in Old Bethpage. Take the L.I.E. to exit 48 and follow the signs.

▪▪▪▪ OUTSIDE

Bethpage State Park (Take the LIE to exit 44S, the Seaford Oyster Bay Expressway/Route 135. Then take exit 8, Powell Avenue and follow the signs; 516-249-0701 for the park, 516-249-0700 for golf info; www.nysparks.state.ny.us). For golfing aficionados, it doesn't get any better than this. Bethpage offers five 18-hole regulation courses including the leg-endary Bethpage Black, a challenging course designed by renowned golf course architect A.W. Tillinghast. The Black Course weekday fee is $50 for residents (Nassau County); $100 for nonresidents. Weekend fees are slightly higher. The other four color-coded courses, Red, Blue, Green, and Yellow, come with their own unique challenges at a lesser game fee (starts at $36 for residents). The reservation fee for any course is $5.

To up your golf game, Bethpage also features golf clinics, lessons, practice putting greens, a driving range, lounge, pro shop, and clubhouse.

Bethpage is best known for its golf courses, but visitors can also find tennis courts, a bridle path, picnic areas, nature trails, playgrounds, and a polo field. Bethpage Park is open year-round.

Bethpage Miniature Golf (130 Hicksville Road, Bethpage; 516-731-2020; www.batterupli.com). Perhaps with a little practice, the kids may one day be able to play the Bethpage Black Course mentioned above. Here's where to get them started. Batting cages, too. Admission costs $6.

▪▪▪▪ SIGHTSEE

American Airpower Museum (1230 New Highway at Republic Airport Hangar 3, Farmingdale;

631-293-6398; www.americanair
powermuseum.com). The American Airpower Museum reinforces
Long Island's storied aviation
history with a fine collection of
aircraft that includes a vintage
1935 Curtiss-Wright P40 Warhawk
fighter plane to a 1967 General
Dynamics F-111 long-range mach
1.2 supersonic jet. The museum
also hosts actual flights in some
of their vintage aircraft, which
lets you don authentic uniforms
and take to the skies. Open Thurs.
through Sun.

■ ■ ■ ■ WATERFRONT

Belmont Lake State Park (625
Belmont Avenue; Babylon; 631-
667-5055). Belmont Lake Park
features 450 acres of boating,
fishing, biking, horseback riding,
hiking, and cross-country skiing
come winter. It also comes with a
bit of history: it was the former
country estate of August Belmont,
Jr., the horse breeder of Belmont
Park fame. The Belmont mansion
was unfortunately razed in the
1930s.

■ ■ ■ ■ EAT

The Bethpage, Farmingdale, Massapequa, and Babylon area offers
some unique high-quality ethnic
and traditional gastronomic gems.
   The Orient (623 Hicksville
Road, Bethpage; 516-822-1010).

Strip mall Szechuan and Can-
tonese success in Bethpage. For
affordable authentic Chinese cuisine and dim sum. Open daily for
lunch and dinner.
   Popei's Clam Bar (384 North
Wantagh Avenue, Bethpage; 516-
822-9169). This local mini-chain
offers really good seafood, generous portions, and affordable
prices in a casual setting. Entrées
from $13–20. Other locations in
Deer Park, Sayville, and Coram.
   El Paso Taco Grill (505 Conklin
Street, Farmingdale; 516-249-
3600).For authentic Mexican
dishes and superb soft tacos. A
wonderful casual option for lunch
that's easy on the pesos.
   Black Forest Brew Haus (2015
New Highway, Farmingdale; 631-
391-9500; www.blackforestbrew
haus.com). Fun and festive Black
Forest will have you dreaming of
Deutschland. For German and
American fare and their own
brand of Black Forest beer in five
flavors brewed on-site. The German sliders of bratwurst on mini
buns with kraut or red cabbage
($11) are a good way to start.
Ample menu. Good portions. German specialty entrées $16–22.
Steaks, salads, burgers, and
seafood, too. Open daily for
lunch and dinner.
   Nathan's Famous (229 Broad-
hollow Road, Farmingdale; 631-
293-6302; www.nathansfamous

.com). Nathan's hot dogs simply must be mentioned. Take the kids to Old Bethpage Village Restoration in the morning, enjoy lunch at Nathan's, and then catch a few rides at Adventureland afterward (except don't let the kids on the rides too soon after eating!).

Ciao Baby (5074 Sunrise Highway, Massapequa Park; 516-799-5200; www.ciaobabyrestaurant .com). The three-course family-style dinner (about $25 a person) lets you choose three menu items each for appetizer, main, and dessert. Tasty choices include calamari arrabiata for starters; rustic chicken scarpariello with sausage, mushroom, and potato for the main; and icebox cake for dessert. Dinner is presented on one gigantic plate—enough to make any Italian grandma shed a tear of joy. Leftovers are guaranteed. Fun Rat Pack lounge flare. It can get boisterously busy especially on weekends. Also in Commack (204 E. Jericho Turnpike; 631-543-1400).

Glenn's Dinette (23 East Main Street, Babylon; 631-669-9858). For casual diner fare in a fun '50s setting. Cash only. Closed Sun.

Horace & Sylvia's (100 Deer Park Avenue, Babylon; 631-587-5081; www.horaceandsylvia.com). A fine neighborhood eatery that offers inventive and hearty tradi-tional American fare such as stuffed pork chop with Gruyere, shallots, spinach, and proscuitto ($19). Entrées $16–22. Soups, sandwiches, pasta, and pizza, too. Open daily for dinner; Tues. through Fri. for lunch as well.

■ ■ ■ ■ SPECIAL EVENTS AT OLD BETHPAGE VILLAGE RESTORATION

Memorial Day Weekend: Sheep to Shawl Festival.

Summer: Civil War Battle Re-enactments.

Summer and Fall: Old Time Base Ball Matches.

Early October: the Long Island Fair (separate admission applies).

Late October: 1880s Long Island Halloween.

Late November: 1860s Thanksgiving Celebration.

Mid December: Holiday Craft Show.

■ ■ ■ ■ STAY

The Courtyard by Marriot Republic Airport (2 Marriot Plaza just off Route 110 south of the L.I.E., Farmingdale; 631-847-0010; www.marriott.com) leaves you close to Old Bethpage Village Restoration, the Bethpage Golf Course, and Adventureland. Deal rates start as low as $119 a night and average about $150 a night.

▪▪▪▪ LIRR OPTION/ LOCAL TAXI INFO

Old Bethpage Village Restoration is accessible from the Farmingdale train station (Ronkonkoma branch). Yellow Cab (516-249-1212) provides service for about $9.

▪▪▪▪ FYI

The prestigious U.S. Open golf tournament was held at the Bethpage State Park Black Course in 2002 and 2009. Tiger Woods won in 2002; Lucas Glover won in 2009.

The U.S. Open golf tournament was also held on Long Island at the Shinnecock Hills Golf Club most recently in 2004, 1995, 1986, and way back when in 1886 (it was the second U.S. Open tournament).

▪▪▪▪ READS AND RESOURCES

Believe it or not. Read *The Amityville Horror: A True Story,* Jay Anson's 1977 novel about a family who move into a typical Long Island suburban home only to be terrorized and chased out by strange goings-on less than a month later. Six family members of the previous occupants were shot and killed in the residence.

Rent *Adventureland,* the 2009 comedy drama written and directed by Greg Mottola. The film was actually shot at Pittsburgh's Kennywood Amusement Park, but it's based on Mottola's days as an employee of Adventureland in Farmingdale, where he worked in the 1980s.

▪▪▪▪ NEXT STOP

Enjoy some Old Bethpage Village Restoration history by day and some family fun by night at **Adventureland** (2245 Route 110, Farmingdale; 631-694-6868; www .adventureland.us). I don't know of a single Long Islander who has never been to Adventureland, Long Island's version of an amusement park, which offers 16 rides for big kids of all ages and another 10 for tots. It's a fun Long Island rite of passage—you go there as a kid, then a teen, and a few years later, you bring your own kids. It ain't Disney—but it is a nostalgic Long Island institution since 1962. Pay-one-price admission costs about $25 for those 48" and taller; about $21 for those under. Single tickets cost $1 (each ride requires 3 to 5 tickets). Adventureland is open daily Apr. through Sept., and then weekends through the end of Oct.

20 • LONG ISLAND ROAD TRIP: *The Long Island Lighthouse Challenge*

Lovers of Lighthouses to the Front of the Line

There's something sentimentally special about a lighthouse. And there's something equally endearing about the people who love them. How to honor these grand maritime beacons as well as some fine folks? Host a Lighthouse Challenge.

The Long Island Lighthouse Challenge was started in 2005 to promote awareness of these national historical treasures. The goal is trek all across Long Island over the course of a mid-May weekend and visit as many lighthouses as you can. The list varies slightly from year to year, but usually there are about 10 stops (nine lighthouses and one museum) on the itinerary. You have two days to complete the task.

It doesn't cost anything to join, but you do need to pay for your own parking, ferry, admission fees, and a tank or two of gas. So what's the reward? For one, bragging rights. In addition, at each designated lighthouse station, participants receive an official stamped piece of paper that verifies a lighthouse has been visited.

You also receive a lighthouse collectible designed especially for that year—anything from a wooden nickel to a bookmark to a trading card depicting a pretty photo of the lighthouse at hand.

Best of all you get to meet a few fine folks along the way. One such lighthouse aficionado is Bob Allen, who in the past has greeted visitors at the Orient Point/Plum Island check-in point. His great-grandfather, William Follet, was the lighthouse keeper of the Cedar Island Lighthouse from 1917 until it was decommissioned in 1934.

"My great-grandfather was in the lighthouse service for 30 years," Allen said. "He began at the Montauk Lighthouse, moved on to Cedar Island Lighthouse, and he ended his career at the Long Beach Bar Lighthouse."

Allen says the Long Island Lighthouse Challenge is usually held the weekend before Memorial Day. The Challenge is held rain or shine, but the mid-May date along the coastal waters of Long Island sometimes brings with it a heavy dose of fog. And that means you sometimes can't see the lighthouse that you're visiting.

"A good lighthouse tour always depends on the weather," he said. "And this is really light-house weather. You've got rain. You've got fog. And that's why lighthouses were built. If it was beautiful weather all the time, you wouldn't have needed a lighthouse."

Although the foggy weather creates appropriate lighthouse atmosphere, Allen admits he hopes for a sunny weekend come every Lighthouse Challenge.

Allen says that of 1,800 light-houses that once graced the waters of the United States, only 597 remain. The town of Southold, most of Long Island's North Fork, boasts eight light-houses in all.

"That's the most in any town-ship in the United States," Allen said.

Allen loves to share stories about his great-grandfather, whom he never got a chance to meet. One wouldn't know that fact, as Allen channels all of granddad's maritime adventures and family history to all who lend an ear. The topic of conversation ranges from previous generations who were raised on lighthouse property to spotting rumrunners in the days of Prohibition.

"A lighthouse keeper didn't just turn on the light." Allen said. "They observed the waters and assisted with rescues."

The keeper also performed lighthouse upkeep.

"And that's why some light-houses are in a state of disrepair today."

Allen's goal is to raise aware-ness as well as money to preserve these national nautical treasures.

"It's like a voyage back in time," he said. "Lighthouses are a piece of history that should not be lost."

■ ■ ■ ■ INFO

The Long Island Lighthouse Chal-lenge usually takes place the weekend before Memorial Day weekend. The Long Island Light-house Society Web site includes suggested itineraries, admission fees, ferry info, and participating hotels. Allen also hosts free walk-ing tours to the Cedar Island Lighthouse year-round. For more information visit www.lilight housesociety.org.

I attempted the 2009 Light-house Challenge, but a previous commitment meant I only had one day to venture to as many lighthouses as I could. I made it to five stops in all at a leisurely pace. That said, I have visited most of the other lighthouses on different occasions.

And, of course, as soon as I finished writing this chapter, I discovered that due to a lack of volunteers, the Long Island Lighthouse Society cancelled the 2010 Long Island Lighthouse Challenge. Nonetheless, here's a two-day Long Island lighthouse drive itinerary that you can visit any time of year on your own. Check the Web site for future Lighthouse Challenges.

■ ■ ■ ■ LONG ISLAND LIGHTHOUSE TOUR

Day One

START: Breakfast is served at **Thomas' Ham and Eggery** (325 Old Country Road, Carle Place; 516-333-3060), a serious diner for breakfast, brunch, lunch, and dinner. Anything served in a sizzling skillet gets points from me. Friendly service. Cash only. Parking can be challenging. This central Nassau location offers nearby access to the Wantagh Parkway. Venture south and then east along Ocean Parkway to Robert Moses State Park.

VISIT: The **Fire Island Lighthouse** (Robert Moses State Park; 631-661-4876; www.fireisland lighthouse.com). Park at Field 5 and take a short boardwalk stroll to the lighthouse (deer are often spotted nearby). This current 168-foot Fire Island Lighthouse dates to 1858 and is cared for independently by the Fire Island Lighthouse Preservation Society. Tower tours and climbs ($6) offer a great view of Fire Island and the Atlantic Ocean. There's also an on-site museum in the former keepers' quarters and a gift store. Robert Moses beach parking costs $8 or use your Empire Passport. Open daily Apr. through mid-Dec.; weekends during winter. You'll now have to do a bit of

Horton Point Lighthouse

backtracking. Venture north on the Sagtikos Parkway, west along the Northern State Parkway, and north on Route 110 into Huntington Village.

VISIT: The **Huntington Harbor Lighthouse** (Huntington Bay, Huntington; 631-421-1985; www .huntingtonlighthouse.org). Built in 1912, Huntington Harbor Lighthouse is only accessible by guided boat tour, which runs twice monthly June through Sept. Tours take place 11 AM–3 PM, weather permitting. Suggested donations cost $10 for adults, $8 for seniors, and $5 children 5 to 12 (no children under five years old, please). Detailed driving directions are listed on their Web site.

LUNCH: Check Chapter 6 (Huntington) for any number of good lunch options. **Skorpios** (340 New York Avenue, Huntington) offers very good Greek fare, and

American Roadside Burgers (337 New York Avenue, Huntington) is home to some of the best burgers on Long Island. Or, in keeping with the seafaring theme, opt for great roadside-style seafood and a dose of clams and chaos at **The Shack** (1 Stony Hollow Road/Route 25A, Centerport, see Chapter 5).

VISIT: Head east along Route 25A and make your way to Port Jefferson Harbor to visit the **Old Field Point Lighthouse**, which is located at the end of Old Field Road. It dates to 1869. Unfortunately, there is no public access, but it nonetheless makes a fine photo op for diehard lighthouse fans.

OVERNIGHT: Port Jeff is a good place to overnight as there are many good dining options such as **Fifth Season** (34 East Broadway, Port Jefferson) for inventive

*Orient Point
Plum Island
Lighthouse*

East End
Seaport
Museum

American cuisine; a grand hotel in **Danford's Hotel and Marina** (25 East Broadway); and lively theater performances at **Theatre Three** (412 Main Street). Don't forget to save some time, pull up a park bench, and kick back by the dock to watch the Port Jeff/ Bridgeport ferry come and go.

Day Two

START: If indeed staying overnight in Port Jeff, enjoy breakfast at **Toast Coffeehouse** (242 East Main Street), the best little resto in town. Venture east along Route 25A to Route 25 and then to County Road 48 on the North Fork of Long Island. Turn north on Youngs Avenue, turn right on Old North Road, and then a quick left on Lighthouse Road.

VISIT: **Horton Point Lighthouse** (Lighthouse Road,

Southold; 631-765-2101). Commissioned by President George Washington in the late 1700s, the structure dates to 1857. Its beacon still provides assistance to mariners. The grounds, which offer beautiful views of the Long Island Sound, are open daily; the on-site museum ($4) is open weekends in summer.

VISIT: Head farther east along Route 25 to the end of the North Fork to Orient Point for a visit to the **Orient Point Plum Island Lighthouse**. Park near the Orient Point/New London ferry and take a short 15-minute hike along the well-marked trail at neighboring Orient Point County Park. The lighthouse is known as "the coffeepot." You can get close from the nearby rocky shoreline, but you can't access it directly as it's surrounded by water.

VISIT: Adjacent to the ferry lot, access Orient Beach State Park (Route 25, Orient; 631-323-2440; www.nysparks.state.ny.us) for a drive-by glimpse of the **Long Beach Bar Lighthouse** located along Gardiners Bay, the body of water that separates the North and South Forks. This replica lighthouse is also known as Bug Lighthouse.

LUNCH: Make your way back to Greenport (see Chapter 8) for a number of excellent lunch options including the casual **BBQ Bill's Famous Texas Barbecue** (47 Front Street). Treat yourself to an authentic nautical souvenir at **S. T. Prestons & Sons** (102 Main Street).

VISIT: The **East End Seaport Museum** (adjacent to the Shelter Island Ferry; 631-477-2100) offers magnificent maritime might for a very nominal fee—$2.

SET SAIL: Take the Greenport/Shelter Island North Ferry (about $9 for car and driver) to Shelter Island. Continue south along Route 114 to the Shelter Island/Sag Harbor South Ferry ($12) and take that ferry to Sag Harbor.

VISIT: From Sag Harbor, make your way to Cedar Point Park in East Hampton for a visit to the **Cedar Point Lighthouse** (5 Cedar Point Road; 631-852-7620). The lighthouse is visible from the bluff. An optional up-close view will take about a 90-minute walk. Then make your way to Route 27/Montauk Highway and head east.

VISIT: The **Montauk Lighthouse** (Montauk Point State Park; 631-668-2544). I can't think of a better way to end a lighthouse tour than with a visit to the Montauk Lighthouse, truly a wonderful landmark and grand symbol of Long Island. The site features an excellent museum space and a 137-step climb to the top of the tower. Admission costs $8.50 for adults. Parking costs $8 (see Chapter 13 for more info).

▪ ▪ ▪ ▪ READS AND RESOURCES

Read Long Island Lighthouses Past and Present by Robert G. Müller.

▪ ▪ ▪ ▪ FYI

Avid lighthouse enthusiasts can also join the Maryland Lighthouse Challenge in mid-Sept. and the New Jersey Lighthouse Challenge in mid-Oct. If the Long Island version makes its return, the trio is known as the **Lighthouse Triple Crown**.

21 • ROADSIDE ATTRACTION IN FLANDERS: *The Big Duck*

Flanders, The Moriches, Eastport, Westhampton, Hampton Bays, Manorville, Quogue

The infamous Big Duck has been a Long Island roadside attraction since 1931. Devoted duck docent Babs Bixby has been a "duck sitter" since the summer of 1993. It came to her attention that the Big Duck was to reopen not as a duck farmer's poultry store, its original incarnation, but as a cute little souvenir shop. She's been there ever since.

"The Big Duck was built by an ordinary duck farmer," Bixby said. "It was an advertising gimmick and a fast food take-out place. You could get roasted Pekin ducklings to go."

Bixby says that at the height of the duck farming industry during the 1930s, Long Island boasted some 90 duck farms in all. Today the Big Duck stands as a souvenir shop that retails everything from shot glasses and refrigerator magnets to T-shirts and coffee mugs. All of these "duck-a-bilia" are rung up on an antique cash register.

"The Big Duck highlights the bygone days of the duck farm," Bixby said. "But the ongoing theme is goofy architecture."

Bixby says first owner Martin Maurer and his wife traveled to California at the height of the Great Depression. Along the way he was inspired by the likes of other roadside attractions such as the Tail o' the Pup hot dog stand and the Brown Derby restaurant.

"So he came back to Long Island and he built this giant duck," Bixby said.

The Big Duck brochure states the duck measures 30 feet long "from beak to perky tail," stands 15 feet wide "from folded wing to folded wing," and stands 20 feet tall.

The Big Duck has moved four times in its eight-decade history. It was first situated in Riverhead on Route 25 during the 1930s. It then stood for some 50 years along Route 24 in Flanders (its current home as well). The Big Duck, in danger of being demolished, was saved from the wrecking ball and moved near Sears Bellows County Park just down the road when it was acquired by Suffolk County in 1988. It opened as a gift shop in 1993 and was moved back to this location, its second home, in 2007.

"It's all duck-umented," quips Bixby.

What's the enduring attraction of this attraction?

"To this day it's hard to put your finger on it," Bixby said. But she offers her own theory she calls "the five As."

"It's an example of wonderful outrageous architecture, advertising, agriculture, in the all-American, automotive age," she said. "It's very folkloric."

Bixby loves to poke fun and enjoy any number of plays on words.

"Duck in and take a gander," she tells visitors. "Don't forget to visit the east and west wing."

Bixby doesn't have an actual count of visitors, but she says it's very well attended.

"It's enough visitors that it's recognized on the National Register of Historic Places."

Bixby says the guests come from all over the world. Some folks stumble upon the Big Duck and wander in with a perplexed expression.

"But most know we're here."

Bridal parties stop by for a memorable wedding day photo op. Celebrities have visited, too, on their way to the Hamptons. Alec Baldwin, Diane Keaton, and Christie Brinkley have all stopped by.

"The appeal of the Big Duck is simply poetic," Bixby said. "It's a fascination. It's a small wonder. It's a pure fun Long Island destination."

▪▪▪▪ INFO

The Big Duck gift store is open daily 10 AM–5 PM Memorial Day through Labor Day (it's closed for lunch from about 1 to 1:30 PM). It's then open weekends only Labor Day through Nov. Call 631-852-8290.

▪▪▪▪ GETTING THERE

The Big Duck is at Route 24 (Flanders Road) in Flanders. Take the L.I.E. to exit 71. Take Route 24 south for about 4 miles. At the traffic circle, take the Flanders Road/Route 24 exit for about 2½ miles. The Big Duck is on your left.

▪▪▪▪ OUTSIDE

Sears Bellows County Park (Bellows Pond Road, Hampton Bays; 631-852-8290; www.co.suffolk.ny .us). A short drive down the road from the Big Duck, Sears Bellows offers hiking, rowboat rentals, camping, picnicking, freshwater fishing, bridle paths, and a tranquil photo op. Use your Suffolk County GreenKey for reduced admission.

Long Island Skydiving Center (91 Montauk Hwy, East Moriches; 631-235-9968; www.longisland skydiving.com). Talk about a view! Daredevils and thrill seekers to the front of the line. The name says it all. Tandem freefall sky-dives cost $219 on weekends; $209 on weekdays. And away we goooooooooooooooo!

Quogue Wildlife Refuge (3 Old Country Road, Quogue; 631-653-4771; www.quoguewildliferefuge .com). This important 305-acre wildlife preserve offers hiking trails as well as a Distressed Wildlife Complex, which aids and cares for injured wild animals. The trails and the Distressed Wildlife Complex are open daily

from sunrise to sunset. The Nature Center Building, which offers exhibitions and a chil-dren's room, is open Tues., Thurs., and weekends 11 AM—4 PM.

■■■■ SIGHTSEE

Animal Farm Petting Zoo (296 Wading River Road, Manorville; 631-878-1785; www.afpz.org). Run by the Long Island Zoologi-cal Society, Animal Farm Petting Zoo is home to resident baby pigs, cows, goats, lambs, bun-nies, monkeys, and more—oh my! Their Zoo Rescue program helps abused, abandoned, and unwanted animals. Open daily. $13.50 for adults; $11.50 for chil-dren and seniors.

■■■■ WATERFRONT

Cupsoque Beach County Park (Dune Road, Westhampton Beach; 631-852-8111; www.co.suffolk.ny .us). Cupsoque offers Atlantic Ocean swimming (with lifeguards on duty), as well as bay-side scuba diving—the water is only 12 feet deep. It's also a popular spot for bluefish and saltwater bass fishing. Campers and RVs are permitted.

Silly Lily Fishing Station (99 Adelaide Avenue, East Moriches; 631-878-0247; www.sillylily.com). Great name! Fun outdoor water adventures. This full-service marina offers fishing boat, kayak,

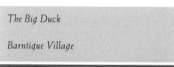

The Big Duck

Barntique Village

and sailboat rentals as well as sailing lessons.

▪▪▪▪ EAT

Moriches Bay Diner (62 Montauk Highway, Moriches; 631-878-6827). The epitome of a superb Long Island diner.

Tavern on Main (361 Main Street, Center Moriches; 631-878-1820; www.tavernonmain restaurant.com). Formerly Moriches Steak House, Tavern on Main offers steak and seafood fare. Open daily for dinner.

Starr Boggs (6 Parlato Drive, Westhampton Beach; 631-288-2573; www.starrboggs.com). Trendy Starr Boggs kicks seafood up a notch. It's not a cheap date, but it is first rate. Monday Night Lobster Bake ($65) includes appetizer, raw bar buffet, steak, lobster, and dessert. A $30 prix fixe is offered Tues. through Thurs. and Sun. Open daily for dinner.

Annona (112 Riverhead Road, Westhampton Beach; 631-288-7766; www.annona.com).
Pricey but carefully executed contemporary American fare and Italian dishes. Refined atmosphere, clean contemporary design, fresh local ingredients. Save this one for a special occasion. Entrées from $28–48.

Edgewater Restaurant (295 East Montauk Highway, Hampton Bays; 631-723-2323; www.edge waterrestaurant.com). A popular spot with the locals—and that's always a culinary good thing. For bountiful appetizers such as pistachio gnocchi in a pesto cream sauce ($11); finely prepared entrées such as shrimp oreganata and risotto ($24); thin-crust pizza and focaccia ($12–19); and steaks and seafood, too. Open daily July and Aug.; Tues. through Sun. the rest of the year; closed Feb.

Eastport Luncheonette (497 Montauk Highway, Eastport; 631-325-8887). The easygoing place for a well-deserved lunch break from your morning antiques shopping in Eastport.

▪▪▪▪ SHOP

These entries are all about East End antiquing. Main Street/ Montauk Highway from Bellport to Amagansett enjoys a variety of antiques shops. There are more than two dozen shops and collectives in all that specialize in furniture, fine art, bric-a-brac, and collectibles. The dealers run throughout the East End and South Fork (and it seems the farther east you go toward the Hamptons, the pricier the antiquities get). The Moriches area and Eastport are a good place to start. Warning: empty the car trunk prior to arrival.

Barntique Village (Montauk Highway, Moriches; 631-878-

4594). For one-stop antiques shopping and some pretty good bargains, nothing comes close. Unique Barntique boasts a collection of a dozen and a half independent antiques sellers and dealers conveniently located in one "village" lot located in Moriches just off Montauk Highway. The village is quite fun to stroll about and browse inside the actual barns. There is no proper Web site, but one dealer, Auntie Q's, does maintain her own blog, which is worth a look at www.willowcontinuation .blogspot.com. Treat yourself to a snack of fresh fruit or homemade baked treats next door at **LaCorte's Farm Stand** (339 Montauk Highway; 631-878-9093).

There are also a number of fine antiques stores in Eastport Village as well. The first stop is **Beyond the Beaten Path** (495 Montauk Highway; 631-325-2105;

www.beyondthebeatenpath.net), run by the ever-engaging Emily Weiss since 1994. She specializes in antiques, jewelry, and vintage clothes and even rents theater costumes.

Also nearby is **KC Kollections** (511 Montauk Highway; 631-325-1845) for lamp shades and more; **Victoria's** (486 Montauk Highway; 631-325-1280); and **Lloyd's Antiques** (496 Montauk Highway; 631-325-1819) for two full floors of fun antiques.

■■■■ SPECIAL EVENTS

Early June: Greater Westhampton Spring Arts & Crafts Show.

Early August: **Greater Westhampton Chamber of Commerce Mary O. Fritchie Outdoor Juried Art Show**. Both at the Westhampton Beach Village Green at Mill Road between Main Street and Church Lane.

Sears Bellows County Park

The first Wednesday in December: the Annual **Holiday Lighting of the Big Duck.** My, that duck looks festive in garland and colored lights!

▪ ▪ ▪ ▪ AFTER DARK

Westhampton Beach Performing Arts Center (76 Main Street, Westhampton Beach; 631-288-1500; www.whbpac.org). The East End venue for theater, dance, performance, film, children's shows, and summer camps. Performances run the gamut from the New York City Opera to *The Velveteen Rabbit,* Loudon Wainwright III to funnyman Louis C.K.

▪ ▪ ▪ ▪ DRIVING TIPS

Because it's there. If you really want to venture to the Big Duck but don't have a car, renting a car for the day may be a less expensive option than taking the train and then cabbing it. The LIRR option is best if you're staying put in Westhampton Beach or Hampton Bays. Keep in mind that the Big Duck visit is pretty much a photo op and a quick peek inside. That said, it's one roadside attraction and slice of Americana that you can cross off your to-do list.

Don't miss a drive along Dune Road, where you can admire some unique oceanfront architecture.

In the area, Main Street doubles as Montauk Highway.

▪ ▪ ▪ ▪ STAY

Westhampton Beach and Hampton Bays enjoy a fair share of comfortable B&Bs. Of note is the **Grassmere Inn Bed and Breakfast** (7 Beach Lane, Westhampton Beach; 631-288-4021). The moderately priced inn is just a half mile from the Westhampton Beach Performing Arts Center. If you prefer an ocean view and larger accommodations, **Dune Deck Hotel** (379 Dune Road, Westhampton Beach; 631-288-3876; www.dune deck.com) is right on the Atlantic Ocean. Summer rates start at $279 a night. For Hampton Bays stays, try the Victorian-style **Inn Spot on the Bay** (32 Lighthouse Road, Hampton Bays; 631-728-1200; www.innspot.com).

▪ ▪ ▪ ▪ LIRR OPTION/ LOCAL TAXI INFO

Westhampton Beach is accessible from the Westhampton Beach train station (Montauk branch). VIP Taxi (631-288-8294) and J.R. West Hampton Taxi (631-728-5100) provide area taxi service. Hampton Bays is accessible from the Hampton Bays station one stop west. Lindy's Taxi (631-283-1900) provides area service.

■■■■ **FYI**

The changing Long Island landscape. The Great Hurricane of 1938 wreaked havoc and caused many deaths on Long Island, particularly in the East End. Dune Road in Westhampton, and many of its oceanfront houses, was pretty much wiped out. The surging waters of the storm actually separated Montauk Point for a short while until the waters receded. The rising waters also created the Shinnecock Inlet, which now connects the Atlantic Ocean to Shinnecock Bay. The inlet is now the easternmost of five inlets that connect the Atlantic Ocean to any number of south shore bays along some 100 miles of barrier beach islands.

The others from west to east are Rockaway Inlet, Jones Inlet, Fire Island Inlet, and Moriches Inlet.

■■■■ **READS AND RESOURCES**

Visit the Greater Westhampton Chamber of Commerce at www .whbcc.com.

Visit the **Hampton Bays Chamber of Commerce** at www .hamptonbayschamber.com.

A great Web resource is **Hamptons Travel Guide** at www .hamptonstravelguide.com.

■■■■ **NEXT STOP**

Stick to the South Shore and head west for a Connetquot Park hike (see Chapter 16), or head east for a South Fork Hamptons tour (see Chapter 12).

APPENDIX: *Everything Else You Need to Know*

▪▪▪▪ LONG ISLAND INFO

Long Island Convention & Visitors Bureau and Sports Commission (330 Motor Parkway, Suite 203, Hauppauge, N.Y. 11788; 877-FUN-ON-LI or 1-877-586-6654; www.discoverlongisland.com)

▪▪▪▪ NASSAU COUNTY INFO

Nassau County Government: Call the Nassau County Operator at 516-571-3000. Visit www.nassaucountyny.gov.

▪▪▪▪ NASSAU COUNTY LEISURE PASS

The Leisure Pass provides proof of residency and reduced admission at Nassau County Parks. It costs $25.

The Leisure Pass is available at Cantiague Park in Hicksville, Christopher Morley Park in Roslyn, Eisenhower Park in East Meadow, Grant Park in Hewlett, Nickerson Beach Park in Lido, North Woodmere Park in North Woodmere, and Wantagh Park in Wantagh.

▪▪▪▪ SUFFOLK COUNTY INFO

Suffolk County Government (www.co.suffolk.ny.us)

The GreenKey pass provides proof of Suffolk County residency

Old Westbury Gardens

and reduced admission at Suffolk County Parks. It costs $20 for adults; $9 for seniors.

A GreenKey pass is available at the West Sayville Park Operations Office; county golf courses (Bergen Point, Indian Island, Timber Point, West Sayville); and parks (Blydenburgh, Cathedral Pines, Cedar Point, Cupsogue, Indian Island, Meschutt Beach, Sears Bellows, Shinnecock East, Smith Point, Southaven, and Theodore Roosevelt).

A nonresident Tourist Reservation Key card is also available for golf and camping access.

▌▌▌▌ NEW YORK STATE INFO

I Love NY Tourism (1-800-CALL-NYS; www.iloveny.com).

New York State Office of Parks, Recreation and Historic Preservation—Long Island Regional Office (625 Belmont Ave., West Babylon, NY 11704; 631-669-1000; www.nysparks.state.ny.us/regions/long-island)

▌▌▌▌ EMPIRE PASSPORT

The Empire Passport provides access (per carload) to 178 state parks and 55 Department of Environmental Conservation forest preserve areas, as well as boat launch sites, arboretums, and park preserves. The sticker costs about $65 and is valid from April through the following March. It's available at most state parks, including Jones Beach. For telephone orders call (in Albany) 518-474-0458.

▌▌▌▌ LONG ISLAND PUBLIC TRANSPORTATION

For **Long Island Railroad** schedule information call 516-822-LIRR or visit www.lirr.org.

For bus information call 516-228-4000.